POVERTY AND MALNUTRITION IN LATIN AMERICA

POVERTY AND MALNUTRITION IN LATIN AMERICA

Early Childhood Intervention Programs

A Report to the Ford Foundation

Ernesto Pollitt

With the Collaboration of
Robert Halpern
and Patricia Eskenasy

PRAEGER

PRAEGER SPECIAL STUDIES • PRAEGER SCIENTIFIC

Library of Congress Cataloging in Publication Data

Pollitt, Ernesto.
    Poverty and malnutrition in Latin America.

    Bibliography: p.
    1. Children--Latin America--Case studies.
2. Malnutrition in children--Latin America--Case
studies. 3. Poor--Latin America--Case studies.
I. Halpern, Robert, 1951-   joint author.
II. Eskenasy, Patricia, joint author. III. Ford   LCAF
Foundation. IV. Title.
HQ792.L3P64   305.2'3'098   80-18811
    ISBN 0-03-058031-5

Published in 1980 by Praeger Publishers
CBS Educational and Professional Publishing
A Division of CBS, Inc.
521 Fifth Avenue, New York, New York 10017 U.S.A.

0123456789 145 987654321

Printed in the United States of America

PREFACE

In December 1976 the Office of Latin America and the Caribbean, International Division of the Ford Foundation, New York, commissioned a comprehensive review of empirical research on early childhood education and human development in Latin America. The instructions were to review documents on the relationships between intervention strategies and malnutrition, sociocultural settings, mental development, and behavior; and to conduct an in depth field study of the development of policy and programs in at least two Latin American countries.

This book is the result of the Foundation's assignment. On a few subjects, it may provide more detail than requested; on others, it may be short of the target. In keeping with Foundation interests, however, the report is an attempt to bridge the gap between research data and public policy. In addition, the discussions of specific issues relating to intervention programs, their cost, and possible effects should be of special interest to policy makers.

The report includes a literature review of documents from the regions and countries studied, as well as three case studies from direct field observations in Puno, Peru; Antioquia, Colombia; and Caracas, Venezuela.

Although the literature review is focused on South America, particularly on studies from five of the seven Andean countries (Chile, Colombia, Ecuador, Peru, and Venezuela), data from studies in Mexico, Jamaica, and Guatemala have been selectively included. The unifying criterion among all of these countries is their high degree of both absolute and relative poverty.

While there exists a wide array of studies on populations in Argentina, Uruguay, and Brazil that are relevant to our present concerns, these countries were excluded from the literature search for several reasons. Argentina, the most highly industrialized country on the continent, and Uruguay were excluded because the presence of absolute poverty is relatively low; Brazil was excluded because it has a language, cultural heritage, and sociopolitical history different from the other countries studied. Literature from other South American countries, such as Bolivia or Paraguay, was not available to the author.

A field study in Caracas was carried out by Patricia Eskenasy, a Venezuelan student at the Department of Nutrition and Food Science at the Massachusetts Institute of Technology in Cambridge, Massachusetts. Robert Halpern, a Ph.D. from the Department of Education at Florida State University, carried out the work in Puno. The Puno section of this study was a part of his doctoral dissertation which focused on the Early Childhood Education Program in Peru. The author conducted the study on Antioquia, Colombia.

A lack of statistics and evaluation data relevant to the programs studied constitutes a serious methodological problem, one which limits the scope of this report to presenting a partial picture of program effectiveness. The report does identify areas in which information is lacking, however, and should serve as a guide to those working to complete the picture.

ACKNOWLEDGMENTS

Many individuals in the United States, as well as in Colombia, Peru, and Venezuela, actively participated in the preparation of this monograph. Although I express my deepest appreciation to them all, I regret that many must remain anonymous.

Robert Myers and Richard Krasno of the Ford Foundation were the major architects who transformed the idea into action. I appreciate their trust in my ability to carry out the project. Eloisa de Lorenzo, Merrill S. Read, Henry Ricciuti, and Horacio Rimoldi were members of the Advisory Group set up by the Foundation for the purposes of this study. Their constructive criticisms, suggestions, and guidelines were invaluable. But obviously I remain totally responsible for the final report.

Robert Halpern prepared the chapter on Puno and also worked diligently on the preparation of other chapters. I learned much from him. Patricia Eskenasy prepared the chapter on Caracas with a true dedication. Carol Thomson and Beverly Stellato-Reitz worked with me from the very beginning, selecting bibliographic materials, cataloguing, and preparing early drafts. Mari Jane Garand typed my notes and half-edited manuscripts with superb patience and ability. Finally, Peggy Amante worked her way through each chapter, editing them with an artful command of language. I owe much to her.

CONTENTS

LIST OF TABLES AND FIGURES

Un pedazo de pan, tampoco habrá ahorá para mi?
Ya no más he de ser lo que siempre he de ser,
pero dadme
una piedra en que sentarme,
pero dadme,
por favor, un pedazo de pan en que sentarme,
pero dadme
en español
algo, en fin, de beber, de comer, de vivir, de reposarse,
y despues me iré . . .
Hallo una extraña forma, esta muy rota
y sucia mi camisa
y ya no tengo nada, esto es horrendo.

Cesar Vallejo, Poemas Humanos

1
POVERTY IN SOUTH AMERICA: MAGNITUDE OF THE PROBLEM

Poverty can be defined in both relative and absolute terms. Those who use the former definition hold that society is divided into various layers and that each layer receives a certain portion of available income. Inequality refers to the extent to which the income share of groups differs from their population share. In this context, poverty generally refers to the lower socioeconomic segments of the population, which receive the smallest share of the total income available (see Ahluwalia, 1975; Rein, 1970; Townsend, 1970).

The latter view is that poverty is an absolute condition, one in which the monetary resources available are insufficient for the purchase of goods and services necessary for subsistence. This approach faces a serious conceptual problem. While there is a consensus that poverty exists below the level of income required to purchase subsistence goods and services, there is no consensus as to the nature and amount of goods and services which should be included in that category. For example, food is regarded universally as a necessity, but questions concerning quantity and quality are answered variously. Food requirements depend on a number of factors, among them an individual's age, sex, activity level, body size, and health status (Gross and Underwood, 1972). Climate, geographic location, and cultural norms also may affect the selection of food required. Thus, subsistence standards depend upon the importance assigned to specific factors and may be modified as income levels change. Subsistence levels generally are relative to such things as the cost of living and the availability of services within a given society. The elasticity of a need fluctuates according to the income of an individual, household, or group of people. Paradoxically, then, what may have been termed absolute poverty may also be regarded as a relative condition.

Despite problems of interpretation, the concept of absolute poverty is useful because it helps define priorities for intervention and points out segments of the population whose health and nutrition, among other needs, are at risk. In the case of children, it identifies groups that are in danger of failing to thrive in terms of growth and development. Turning to the problem of poverty in South America, an attempt is made in the following paragraphs to outline the magnitude and severity of the condition in the less industrialized countries on the continent.

INEQUALITY AND POVERTY IN
SOUTH AMERICA

Tables 1 and 2 present income distribution data and per capita GNP for nine South American countries, including Panama. In the publication from which these data were obtained (Ahluwalia, 1975) the author had divided the countries into high, moderate, and low levels of inequality according to the percent of the total income shared by the lowest 40 percent of the population. Table 1, which includes Uruguay, Chile, and Argentina, refers to countries where the income share of the lowest 40 percent of the population is above 12 percent, but below 18 percent of the total. This range represents moderate inequality. Table 2, which includes six countries, indicates that the lowest 40 percent of the population shares less than 12 percent of the total income. This defines a state of high inequality. No South American country exhibits a state of low inequality.

Recent analyses indicate that in most Latin American countries income distribution has become increasingly more inequitable. As national income has expanded, the new increment has tended to go to the middle and upper classes (Frank and Webb, 1977). For example, in Colombia the share of national income of the top 10 percent of the population grew from 41.5 percent to 44.4 percent between 1962 and 1970. The share of the bottom 10 percent decreased from 1.7 percent to 0.8 percent during the same period.

Redistribution policies in Latin America have relied traditionally on wage increases and, to a lesser extent, expenditures on social services. This has applied particularly to education. But wage increases have not affected the bottom 20-30 percent of income earners; the positive effect has been strongest on those already earning above the national average. Harbison (1977) found that formal and nonformal education played only a small part in the distribution of wealth and income in Latin America and other developing countries. The redistribution effect has been minimized by a number of factors that inhibit the poor child's ability to take advantage of the educational system.

TABLE 1

Cross-Classification of Countries by Income Level and Equality
(moderate inequality)

Country (year)	Per Capita GNP US$	Lowest 40 Percent	Middle 40 Percent	Top 20 Percent
Uruguay (1968)	618	16.5	35.5	48.0
Chile (1968)	744	13.0	30.2	56.8
Argentina (1970)	1,079	16.5	36.1	47.4

Note: Share of lowest 40 percent larger than 12 percent and below 18 percent.
Source: Ahluwalia, 1975.

TABLE 2

Cross-Classification of Countries by Income Level and Equality
(high inequality)

Country (year)	Per Capita GNP US$	Lowest 40 Percent	Middle 40 Percent	Top 20 Percent
Ecuador (1970)	277	6.5	20.0	73.5
Colombia (1970)	358	9.0	30.0	61.0
Brazil (1970)	390	10.0	28.4	61.6
Peru (1971)	480	6.5	33.5	60.0
Panama (1969)	692	9.4	31.2	59.4
Venezuela (1970)	1,004	7.9	27.1	65.0

Note: Share of lowest 40 percent less than 12 percent.
Source: Ahluwalia, 1975.

Income distribution data are informative for pointing out the large inequities found within Latin American societies, but they do not illustrate the living conditions of that segment of the population which receives the smallest share of national income. For this purpose, estimates of absolute poverty must be used with the caveat that such estimations, spread across different countries, carry with them an assumption of universality of needs.

Table 3 presents population estimates below two poverty lines; one is set at $50[*] and the other at $75 for 1969 (Ahluwalia, 1975). Both are arbitrary criteria and represent only crude estimates of poverty. In any income scaling for the countries in question, however, it can be assumed that incomes below $50 or $75 will be totally insufficient to meet the needs for food, clothing, shelter, and other vital goods and services.

For illustrative purposes the focus of this analysis may be placed on Ecuador, Colombia, and Peru. When these three countries are combined, nearly eight million people fall below the $50 criterion; that is, 37 percent of the population in Ecuador, 15.4 percent in Colombia, and 19 percent in Peru. Except for Ecuador, which has recently experienced rapid economic growth because of oil resources, there is no reason to believe that there has been a reduction in the number of cases of absolute poverty. Indeed, in Peru, because of the 1977-1978 economic crisis, it can be safely assumed that the number of cases has increased greatly.

The number of children zero to four years that will be living in conditions of extreme poverty in 1980 may be estimated from population projections (Table 4) and from estimates of population below the poverty line (Table 5). Table 5 shows that in 1980 nearly one million children in Colombia and Ecuador, and 800,000 in Peru, will be living in conditions which make it impossible to obtain the basic necessities of food, clothing, and shelter. It is likely that Bolivia may have a problem of similar magnitude.

Note that these crude estimates are based on definitions of extreme poverty (less than $75 per capita). If a higher basal income (less than $150) were used, the number of children would increase considerably, not only in the countries already cited but also in other South American countries such as Venezuela and Chile.

---

[*]All dollar amounts throughout text refer to U.S. dollars.

TABLE 3

Estimates of Population Below Poverty Line in 1969

Country	1969 GNP Per Capita	1969 Population (millions)	Population Below $50		Population Below $75	
			Millions	Percent of Total Population	Millions	Percent of Total Population
Ecuador	264	5.9	2.2	37.0	3.5	58.5
Colombia	347	20.6	3.2	15.4	5.6	27.0
Brazil	347	90.8	12.7	14.0	18.2	20.0
Uruguay	649	2.9	.1	2.5	.2	5.5
Panama	692	1.4	.1	3.5	.2	11.0
Chile	751	9.6	0	0	0	0
Venezuela	974	10.0	0	0	0	0
Argentina	1,054	24.0	0	0	0	0

Source: Ahluwalia, 1975.

5

TABLE 4

Population Projections for Children 0-4 Years
(in thousands)

Countries	1970	1980	
		Number	Percent Growth in 10 Years
Argentina	2,553	2,925	(12.7)
Bolivia	791	1,088	(31)
Brazil	15,132	19,805	(30.8)
Colombia	4,143	5,670	(36.8)
Chile	1,377	1,605	(16.5)
Ecuador	1,130	1,542	(35)
Paraguay	452	650	(44)
Peru	2,371	3,095	(31)
Uruguay	285	318	(11)
Venezuela	1,899	2,532	(33)

Source: United Nations, 1970.

TABLE 5

Estimations of Population of Children (0-4 years old)
Below Poverty Line for 1980
(in thousands)

Country	Estimated Population (1980)	Population Below $50 (percentage)	Population Below $75 (percentage)
Argentina	2,925	0 0	0 0
Bolivia	1,038	data not available	
Brazil	19,805	2,772 (14)	3,961 (20)
Colombia	5,670	873 (15.4)	1,530 (27)
Chile	1,605	0 0	0 0
Ecuador	1,542	570 (37)	902 (58.5)
Paraguay	650	data not available	
Peru	3,095	584 (18.9)	789 (25.5)
Uruguay	318	0 0	0 0
Venezuela	2,532	0 0	0 0

Source: UNICEF/CEPAL, 1979.

2
POVERTY AND COGNITIVE DEVELOPMENT

POVERTY AND EDUCATIONAL ACHIEVEMENT

Formal education contributes to the acquisition of knowledge and skills which are useful in an industrial society; that is, it encourages the development of specific intellectual tools that can be applied in a variety of settings and circumstances (Scribner and Cole, 1973). It is neither the only nor the most powerful socializing influence, but there are sufficient data to support the notion that schooling helps shape modes of cognitive function to fit societal demands (Hall, 1972; Wagner, 1974; Stevenson et al., 1978; Sharp, Cole, and Lave, 1979).

An old yet informative study on the nature of the covariation between educational achievement and poverty was conducted in four Chilean provinces (Hamuy et al., cited in Havinghurst, R. J., 1973) and showed that the drop-out rate of a cohort of children born in 1939 was much higher among rural children than among urban children. The first rural-urban comparison showed that of total first grade enrollment, 53 percent of the urban children and 22 percent of the rural children enrolled in sixth grade. The breakdown by socioeconomic status showed that 80 percent of the children in the high income stratum enrolled, compared to 28 percent of those in the lower income group.

Between 1972 and 1975 the Ministry of Education of Ecuador, in collaboration with the U.S. Agency for International Development (USAID), conducted a sector analysis of elementary education in that country (Reed, 1975). The purpose was to establish a data base for future evaluations, program preparation, and policy planning. Four hundred twenty-nine schools were sampled from a nationwide survey and every first, fourth, and sixth grade student, a total of 26,449, was evaluated. Socioeconomic and intelligence test data and educational achievement scores were collected on most subjects.

In keeping with the Chilean study, this survey also notes a national process of school desertion that is directly related to the socioeconomic characteristics of the pupils. Thus, although free public schooling exists in Ecuador, not all children take advantage of it to the same extent. This pattern is clearly illustrated in a comparison of school enrollment between urban and rural samples, the latter having a significantly higher prevalence of poverty than the former. Of the population entering first grade, the urban schools exhibit a 50 percent retention rate in the sixth grade while the rural schools maintain that rate only into the third grade. Among government supported schools the drop-out rate of rural schools is roughly twice that of urban schools.

The study also showed that in order to keep their children in school, the poor devote a greater proportion of their income to school-related expenses than do those who are financially better off. It is not surprising, then, to find that desertion in the early grades is partly a result of the inability of the parents to pay for textbooks and uniforms. Furthermore, the children of the poor generally attend schools which are likely to have administrative and organizational problems; for example, in urban schools nearly all teachers work with one grade, in rural schools only a third of them do so.

It is important to note that the rural-urban differences in access to educational systems in South America particularly affect the native Indians, who constitute a poverty-stricken rural population. In Peru, for example, fewer Quechua than Spanish-speaking children complete first grade. This difference is likely to be related to the initial language barrier faced by Quechua children and the fact that there are few schools in the areas inhabited by the Quechuas. In keeping with this difference, it is not surprising that the prevalence of illiteracy is noticeably higher in the rural areas (40 percent) than in the urban areas (22 percent), and in the native Indian population than in the Spanish-speaking population (USAID/Peru, 1975).

A study conducted in the municipality of Gachancipa, a small rural region near Bogota, Colombia, also demonstrated that children who drop out of school differ in many ways from those who remain in school (Drysdale, 1972). The study included a number of interesting analyses, but comment will be limited to a review of the comparisons between those children who were enrolled in the fourth and fifth grades and those children who dropped out between the first and fifth grade (see also Drysdale, 1974).

Drysdale focused on 435 children and on the economic and social characteristics of their families. On the basis of discrete family variables, a first between-group comparison showed that 14 out of 20 variables differentiated the two groups in question. In comparison to those children who withdrew from school, the children who remained were more likely to come from families which were financially better off; to have parents with higher levels of schooling; to live closer to school; and to "have a better breakfast" (not defined). In light of this last finding, it is not surprising that the schooled children were heavier and taller than those who withdrew. As expected, there were also significant differences between groups in achievement test scores.

Data reviewed for four Andean countries (Chile, Colombia, Ecuador, and Peru) are in agreement with one another and point out that poverty is an obstacle to educational promotion and achievement. It is not unreasonable, then, to assume that the selective cognitive benefits derived from the educational process are not easily obtained by a child in an impoverished environment. It would be naive to expect, however, that with greater access to formal education all the developmental and cognitive problems of poor children would disappear.

In many of the Andean countries, schools for the rural and urban poor are far from satisfactory. They often overemphasize rote learning and submissive attitudes, have no understanding of the child's family conditions, and may even disregard or possibly derogate the child's cultural heritage. Castillo (1975), in a book on Peruvian children, cogently and succinctly describes educational problems of the poor child which have existed for decades. The following is an edited version of that section of the book:

Peruvian education needs a substantive change, even if this change requires decades. Children in the cities and in the country go to school to learn about an old and wealthy, beautiful and fair, democratic country. In the end, however, this ideal country, described so many times in different classroom settings, has nothing to do with reality.

The schooling system, an ally of capitalism, withholds information from the children on why human inequities do exist in a country which is said to be a representative democracy. The school avoids an analysis of the social problems of the country, under the pretext of a neutral pedagogical system in which nobody believes.

School does not teach the urban or rural child how to work, or how to cultivate. Instead the school teaches theoretical and practical problems oriented towards the transformation of nature, the roles of countries within history, idealistic concepts, and information of little value, most of which hinder the development of a critical attitude.

By pushing aside the native language of Indian children in the Andean region, or in the Amazon region, and imposing Spanish, the official language of the country, the schools force children to join the Peruvian community having a handicap in their own language.

The child is required to go to school clean, well-dressed, with shoes, and without intestinal parasites, or eczema. In turn, the school wants the child to take with him some mastery of the language, a basic education which is called "good manners and behavior," some topics for conversations and restricted subjects of interest. None of these so-called achievements, however, have anything to do with Peruvian reality. The school wants the child to learn how to use electricity, hygienic services, a tooth brush, but it forgets that 33% of the total population do not have potable water, and that 27% do not have latrines. It doesn't remember, either, that many of the children go to school do not have enough money to buy tooth paste, soap and shoes.

POVERTY AND DEVELOPMENTAL/INTELLIGENCE TEST SCORES

The following review is arranged according to the ages of the children included in the studies discussed. Most research has focused on subjects whose ages fall at the end of the preschool period; there is a scarcity of information on the developmental characteristics of infants and toddlers. Because of this limited information, and in order to make it more comprehensive, the review also includes data on children who are beginning primary schooling.

In Santiago, Chile, a group of psychologists (Rodriguez et al., 1976) has standardized a psychomotor scale for the evaluation of 0- to 24-month-old infants. Its roots are found in the Gesell Schedule, but the nature of the subtests and their sequence have been modified to meet cultural demands imposed by the Chilean context. In its present form the scale measures four different developmental areas: motor, language, social, and intersensory organization.

For standardization purposes 600 infants were tested. This sample included an equal number of infants from upper-middle and low income backgrounds. The ages of the infants included in both samples increased monthly from 1 to 12 months; thereafter, it included infants 15, 18, 21, and 24 months old.

Cross-sectional comparisons were made between the developmental quotients (DQ) of the two income groups at all 16 age points. Statistically significant differences in the developmental quotients and in the expected direction were found at 2, 18, 21, and 24 months of age; however, the between-group differences at two months of age were numerically very small in comparison to the substantive differences found at 18 and 24 months. Indeed, at two months of age the difference between groups is solely determined by the differences in the motor area; there were no differences in the three other developmental areas of the scale. At 18 months, three out of the four areas tested differed between groups (motor, intersensory coordination, and language); at 24 months the DQ differences were restricted to language. At eight and at nine months the infants of the middle group performed better than the low socioeconomic group in the motor and language areas, respectively (Rodriguez and Lira, 1976; Lira and Rodriguez, 1976), but at neither age were there between-group differences in the developmental quotients.

In summary, it is apparent that although there may have been some developmental differences between groups during the first 15 months of life, these differences were relatively small, were not stable, and were probably limited to the motor area. At 18 and 24 months, group differences in language became apparent as did the significant differences in the aggregate developmental quotients. At 18 months, for example, the range of difference reached as much as 30 DQ points.

The significance of these data in terms of the later development of the children is unknown. The predictive validity of the developmental scales is poor; as the test-retest time interval increases, the correlations of coefficients between scores approximates zero (McCall, 1979). This is particularly true when first and second testing occur in infancy and adolescence, respectively; however, predictive power of socioeconomic status for level of intelligence function is high if the socioeconomic status remains relatively stable. Accordingly, if the children of low-income parents remain in the same impoverished environment throughout their development, it can be validly assumed that low intelligence test performance observed in early life will remain in later childhood or adolescence (McCall, 1977, 1979).

Following this same line of research, which contrasts the intelligence test performance of children from markedly different income groups, we find another Chilean study carried into the third year of life. Monckeberg et al. (1972), in a study concerned with malnutrition and mental development, compared the growth and psychomotor development of 220 children from a slum area in Santiago with that of 90 middle-class children. Among the low-income group, half of the children were between one and three years of age, and half were four or five years of age. For the high-middle income group, 42 children fell in the younger age range. The younger children in both samples were tested with the Gesell Schedules, while the older children took the Terman Merrill Intelligence Scale.

Results of the tests showed that overall only 26 percent of the low-income subjects obtained a developmental or intelligence quotient within the normal range, whereas 97 percent of the contrasting group had this level of achievement. Examining the results by age, the data showed that 73 percent of the one- to three-year-old children in the low-income sample were classified as either subnormal or deficient, with the areas of language (87 percent) and motor development (54 percent) showing the highest and lowest percentage of cases falling at the subnormal levels. Among the high-middle income group, only three of the one- to three-year-old children were classified as subnormal. In the older group, 78 percent of the low-income sample were either subnormal or deficient, whereas only 2 percent of the contrasting group fell in this category.

One of the most comprehensive studies found on the intelligence level of low socioeconomic children is that of M. Llanos (1974) in Lima. For this study, approximately 300 children 6 to 7 years of age were tested with the Peruvian adaptation of the Wechsler Intelligence Scale for Children (WISC). Half the children attended private schools and were from families of middle or high income (Group A). The remaining children attended public schools, came from slum dwellings in and around Lima, and were classified as being of low socioeconomic status (Group B). Weight and height measures, showing that on the average the children in Group A were taller and heavier than those in Group B, suggest an important difference in their nutritional history. Moreover, among the fathers of the private-school children, 59 percent had completed secondary schooling, and 41 percent had a university degree. In the case of the public-school children, 79 percent of their fathers had completed only primary schooling. A similar between-group difference in educational level existed among mothers of the children in both groups.

Results from the WISC showed that Group A obtained an average IQ of 106.2 (range 81 to 126), which fell in the "average" range of Wechsler's intelligence classification system. The frequency distribution (in percent) for the IQs of both groups for the different levels of the Wechsler intelligence classification paradigm is presented in Table 6.

Following an analysis of the subsets from the WISC, Llanos reports that the children from the squatter settlements who were going to public schools showed deficits in all the cognitive areas that were studied. The only subtests where the performance of these

TABLE 6

Frequency Distribution for Wechsler IQ
(in percent)

IQ Range	Classification Level	Percent Distribution	
		Group A	Group B
60-69	Mentally retarded	0	9.7
70-79	Borderline	0	31.9
80-89	Slow normal	4.8	34.6
90-109	Average	59.8	23.8
110-119	Superior normal	25.8	0
120	Superior	8.0	0

Source: M. Llanos, 1974.

children was at the normal or average level were in Arithmetic, Analogies, and Block Design. In all the other eight subtests their average performance was significantly below statistical expectations. The poorest level of performance was found in Comprehension (making judgments about social situations) and Object Assembly (wood puzzle).

On the basis of the subtest data analysis the author suggests that the three average scores (Arithmetic, Analogies, and Block Design) are evidence that the potential capabilities of these children are in jeopardy because of their environmental limitations. Moreover, she infers from the data on Comprehension and Object Assembly that it is precisely in the areas that tap socialization competence that these children fail. Finally, it is important to note that Llanos did not find any differences between the scores for boys and girls in either group.

Perhaps the strongest evidence on the differences in scores on tests of cognitive development between low- and high-income children is found in data from a longitudinal study conducted in Cali, Colombia, on the effects of comprehensive intervention on chronically deprived children (McKay et al., 1978). Data on the results of the intervention itself will be reviewed in Chapter 4. At this point the focus is restricted to the test performance of the children before exposure to treatment. After the completion of a large survey of impoverished children living in two of the city's lowest-income areas, a sample of 333 children was selected from among 449 subjects. The children were placed in one of four treatment groups. In one group, treatment began when the mean age of the children was about 42 months; in the second group, when the children were about 54 months old; and in the third and fourth groups, when the children were about 64 and 76 months old. The selection criteria for the children in the four groups were the following: (1) lowest height and weight for age of all the children surveyed; (2) highest number of clinical signs of malnutrition; (3) lowest per capita family income.

In addition, two groups of children who received no treatment were included in the study. One group was made up of high-income children and the other of low-income children, and each group exhibited normal weight and height for their chronological age. Except for the low-income children without treatment, all other children were evaluated at the same time points during the study. Evaluations included the administration of short psychological tests, given at different times, that measured language usage, immediate memory, manual dexterity, information and vocabulary, quantitative concepts, spatial relations, and logical thinking. The Stanford-Binet Intelligence Scale was also used in the behavioral appraisal. Analytic studies on the data from the different short tests showed that a similar "general cognitive ability" was evaluated throughout the study.

Prior to the initiation of the comprehensive treatment, behavioral test data for all experimental groups indicated large differences between their scores and the scores of the high-income children. For example, by 60 months of age the mean scaled score on general cognitive ability of the two experimental groups that had received no treatment up to that point was .30 and .22; on the other hand, the mean for the high socioeconomic children was 2.28. Moreover, at the completion of the study the children in the low-income, untreated group had a mean IQ score in the Stanford-Binet of 79.4 (s.d. = 9.72), while the mean for the high-income children was 109.2 (s.d. = 14.86). The particular significance of these data is that they come from a study that has clearly documented that these levels of mental ability are not fixed but extremely malleable. This study has shown that the scores in the tests of cognitive ability among the low-income children can be greatly improved following long-term periods of psychoeducation, nutrition, and health intervention.

A key question in this discussion concerns the relevance of low developmental or intelligence test scores in terms of the future development of the child. Intelligence scales transported from industrialized nations to preindustrial regions of South America may tap irrelevant constructs in terms of the adaptation of the native child to his own ecology and culture. If this is indeed the case, then a low IQ measured at an early age may have no bearing on the life of the child in the hills of Guatemala, or the high altitude in Bolivia or Peru, or in the slum areas of Medellin or Cali in Colombia (Berry, 1974, 1976).

Some data from the longitudinal study at the Institute of Nutrition of Central America and Panama (INCAP) give partial answers to these important questions (Irwin et al., 1978). The subjects of this study were children between 7 and 13 years residing in four villages included in a longitudinal study on food supplementation and cognitive development (see Chapter V). These villages (800 to 1,200 inhabitants) are part of the Spanish-speaking Eastern region of Guatemala where economic activity is primarily agricultural, and family incomes average approximately $300 per year. All children in the study were tested with the preschool battery developed for the longitudinal project. Testing took place within a month of the children's seventh birthday. For the purposes of this study the investigators focused on the composite score of the battery and on the following subtests: Embedded Figures, Digit Span, Picture Vocabulary Recognition, Verbal Analogies, Free Recall Learning, Discrimination Learning, Conservation of Material, and Incomplete Figures.

Each village has a government elementary school with grades from one to six. Although the children in Guatemala can begin school at age seven, they generally register at age eight or older. The schooling data used as outcome variables were obtained from the village teacher's roll books (for years of enrollment) and from the records of the central office of the Ministry of Education in Guatemala City. The school achievement measures are teacher's grades in mathematics and language, averaged across all years of attendance. Complete schooling data for all village children from 1970 through 1975 were available.

Table 7 presents the number of years of school completed by the children in the study sample. Note that among 191 boys there were 73 who had 0 years of education; and among 182 girls there were 71 with no school experience.

A statistical comparison of the preschool test scores between those children who were later enrolled and those who were not showed differences among girls but not among boys. The means for schooled girls in comparison to nonschooled girls were statistically significant for Composite Scores, Embedded Figures, Digit Span, Vocabulary Recognition, Verbal Analogies, and Incomplete Figures. In the case of the boys, schooled and nonschooled children obtained similar scores in all tests. Thus, there seems to be an important interaction between sex and cognitive-type tests of ability in deciding whether a

TABLE 7

Number of Years of School Completed by Children in Study Sample

No. of Years	0	1	2	3	4	5	6	Total
Boys	73	31	25	31	20	15	6	191
Girls	71	17	24	28	22	15	5	182

Source: Irwin et al., 1978.

child goes to school or not. Among boys, these abilities may make no difference; all boys go to school. In the case of the girls, there seems to be a need for evidence of ability before they are enrolled in school. Among boys the correlations between tests and age of enrollment are also suggestive. A negative and significant correlation coefficient was found for the boys between age of enrollment and the composite score ($r = -.30$), Digit Span ($r = .19$), and Conservation of Material ($r = -.39$).* In the case of girls, significant and inverse correlations were found for Composite Score ($r = -.28$), Embedded Figures ($r = -.18$), and Vocabulary Recognition ($r = -.35$). Thus, the greater the evidence of cognitive test competence, the earlier the enrollment in school. The study also demonstrated that, among the girls, the children with higher test scores were also likely to stay in school for a longer period of time.

In terms of the relevance of the preschool period to later educational achievement, the most important data from the study are the correlations between preschool battery performance and school achievement indexes. Among both boys and girls, the cognitive test measurements in the preschool period were relatively good predictors of later grades in mathematics and language.

It is possible that there is no causal relationship between these correlations; that is, the data reported above do not necessarily mean that intelligence was the determinant of enrollment or success in school. An alternate explanation for these findings is that the children with higher cognitive test scores, who are enrolled early in

---

*The coefficients are small, but they are all statistically significant at the .05 level or better; in most cases N > 100 subjects.

school and who obtain high school grades, come from families with social and economic status among the highest in the village. Accordingly, socioeconomic status and not intelligence would be the factor behind the correlations observed. The authors have addressed this issue, and state that the relationships between family characteristics and school success are weak; therefore, in their opinion, the correlations are not spurious. Be that as it may, it is also possible that early enrollment depends upon a series of mental abilities that are valued by the parents because they are recognized as necessary for school success. This simply means that the parents reward the development of certain modes of cognitive operations because, from their knowledge of how these institutions work, they are aware that such modes fit in with school demands. If the children do succeed, then the children are further reinforced and continue their school enrollment.

CONCLUSIONS

From the projections based on demographic and economic data, it may be concluded that, as no major sociopolitical changes have occurred up to the present time, at least three of the Andean countries (e.g., Colombia, Peru, and Ecuador) will have close to one million infants and preschool children (up to four years old) living in conditions of extreme poverty ($50 to $75 per capita). These conditions will markedly restrict the chances these children have to enroll in formal educational institutions. Although these limitations are probably imposed in part by limited availability of schools, it seems likely that the major obstacle to enrollment will be the socioeconomic conditions of the families. Indeed, even if more schools were to become available to children living under conditions of extreme poverty, it does not follow necessarily that there will be a significant increase in enrollment or in the development of mental skills required by industrialized societies. If the socioeconomic characteristics of these families remain unchanged, they are likely to maintain their restriction over the participation of these children in the formal educational process. Furthermore, increments in the number of schools now available for the extremely poor—without improvements in their educational quality—would be of little benefit to these children even if they were to enroll.

All pertinent studies reviewed showed that developmental and intelligence test scores of low-income children often lie significantly behind the scores of children from middle- or high-income families. This differential is usually of considerable magnitude after the children are 19 to 24 months of age, and it is found in areas (for example, language) which are contributors to the development of cognitive skills required by industrialized societies. Studies that analyzed patterns of scores among subtests in the intelligence scales indicate that these differences are symptomatic of differential antecedent experiences, and that the low-income children have the potentiality for the development of such skills and aptitudes. Nevertheless, the initial handicap may jeopardize later school work, as the scores in these intelligence scales are relatively good predictors of later school success.

3
MALNUTRITION AND COGNITIVE
DEVELOPMENT

Chapter 2 established the association between poverty and mental development without analyzing those components of poverty which may have specific adverse effects on cognition. The analysis begins in this chapter as the focus turns to malnutrition and its influence on brain function. In this context malnutrition includes protein-energy malnutrition (PEM), iodine deficiency, and iron deficiency. No attempt is made to examine the effects of other nutrient deficiencies (hypervitaminosis A, for example) because there is a lack of information relating to them.

Available research data show that PEM (Pollitt and Thomson, 1977), iodine deficiency (Greene, 1977), and iron deficiency anemia (Leibel, Greenfield, and Pollitt, 1979) can adversely affect mental development. These nutritional deficiencies are highly prevalent in certain regions of South America and represent serious public health problems (Organizacion Panamericana de la Salud [OPS], 1976). The data on PEM and iodine deficiency are largely derived from studies conducted in Latin America. The data on iron deficiency anemia come primarily from U.S. studies. This review is limited to PEM and iodine deficiency, with a brief note on the putative effects of iron deficiency anemia.

PROTEIN-ENERGY MALNUTRITION (PEM)

Table 8 presents prevalence figures for PEM among Latin American children under five years of age and is divided according to severity and country. Important differences in the nature and size of the samples notwithstanding, these data as a whole are indicative of public health problems of considerable magnitude. In some

TABLE 8

Protein-Energy Malnutrition in South America Among Children Under Five Years of Age

Country or Other Political Unit	Year(s)	Total No. Examined	Percent Normal	Percent Malnourished[a]		
				Degree I (percent)	Degree II (percent)	Degree III (percent)
Bolivia	1966–1969	968	60.1	29.0	10.2	0.7
Brazil	1968	569	31.7	48.4	17.2	2.7
Chile	1977	1,070,707	85.1	11.9	2.5	0.5
Colombia	1966	3,378	33.4	45.6	19.3	1.7
Ecuador	1965–1969	9,000	60.3	28.9	9.6	1.2
Panama[b]	1967	632	39.3	48.8	10.8	1.1
Paraguay	1973	41,750	92.2	4.9	2.2	0.7
Peru	1965–1971	83,165	56.0	32.8	10.9	0.8
Venezuela[c]	1974	23,271	51.1	35.3	12.2	1.4

[a] According to the Gomez Classification.
[b] Estimates based on 1965 population.
[c] Includes children 0–6 years of age.

Sources: UNICEF, Situacion de la Infancia en America Latina y el Caribe No. 49.319, Santiago, Chile, 1979; Organizacion Panamericana de la Salud, 1976.

communities, the combined prevalence for all degrees of severity exceeds 50 percent of the total population (OPS, 1976).

During the past 20 years a large number of studies have been done in Latin America to determine whether or not protein and energy deficiency have adverse effects on cognitive development. A pioneering paper by Cravioto and Robles, in 1965, on the effects of kwashiorkor (protein deficiency) was followed by other reports which investigated the behavioral effects of both severe and mild-to-moderate malnutrition (see review by Pollitt and Thomson, 1977). To facilitate review, these reports are classified here according to: (1) severity of the condition, and (2) experimental design.

A breakdown is provided between studies which focus on severe PEM and those which focus on mild-to-moderate malnutrition. The latter group, in turn, is divided into studies which are strictly correlational and those which are quasi-experimental. This chapter is limited to correlational studies of children with severe (kwashiorkor or marasmus) or mild-to-moderate protein-energy malnutrition; the following chapter reviews quasi-experimental studies.

SEVERE PROTEIN-ENERGY MALNUTRITION:
KWASHIORKOR, MARASMUS, AND UNDIFFERENTIATED

Kwashiorkor is generally a result of inadequate intake of proteins relative to calories. Marasmus arises from inadequate intake of both proteins and calories and, in children, often results in a state of starvation or near starvation. Epidemiologically, kwashiorkor or marasmus are seldom seen in their pure states among severely malnourished children; most cases present signs and symptoms of both conditions or may alternate between the two. This combined condition is sometimes referred to as marasmus-kwashiorkor (Scrimshaw and Behar, 1961; Waterlow and Alleyne, 1971). Waterlow and Rutishauser (1974) have distinguished between growth patterns presumably characteristic of children with each condition. A child with kwashiorkor grows normally for approximately the first six to eight months of life, at which time growth velocity begins to decline. By 14–18 months the child's weight for age has fallen to 60–80 percent of the standard (Boston Growth Norms, in Nelson, Vaughn, and McKay, 1969). Marasmic children, on the other hand, are frequently offsprings of undernourished women, are of low birthweight, show a large weight-for-age deficit even in the first few months of life, and at no time maintain the expected growth velocity for their chronological age. (See also McLaren, 1966, who has made a proposition similar to that of Waterlow and Rutishauser, 1974).

Validation of factors identified as diagnostic of kwashiorkor or marasmus is difficult because few data exist on the premorbid condition of these children, and also because etiologic factors vary with sociocultural practices (including dietary behavior), incidence of infection, and geographic area. Nevertheless, on the basis of an evaluation of available retrospective information and clinical description, several inferences can be made which are pertinent to a discussion of the effects of severe PEM on behavior: (1) marasmus usually develops shortly after birth and, by definition, is chronic; (2) kwashiorkor usually develops in the second year of life and is most likely to be an acute condition; (3) marasmus appears to have multiple etiologic factors while kwashiorkor is more likely to be the result of a dietary deficiency.

Apathy, irritability, anorexia, and withdrawal are the most commonly observed symptoms among kwashiorkor children. Neurological examinations have frequently shown hypotonia, poorly developed motor skills, and, occasionally, cortical and subcortical atrophy (Marcondes et al., 1973). Some researchers were not able to obtain measurable responses on mental development scales from children with severe kwashiorkor (Geber and Dean, 1956).

Reduced activity, hypotonia, cortical atrophy, and reduced brain weight have been reported in children with marasmus (Marcondes et al., 1973; Winick and Rosso, 1969). Also, the marasmic child, unlike the anorexic kwashiorkor child, is often reported to be hungry (McCance and Widdowson, 1966).

Lester and coworkers (1975) tested 12-month-old infants diagnosed as having second- and third-degree malnutrition according to the classification devised by Gomez et al. (1956). These infants and a control group of normal weight infants listened to an intermittent 90-dB tone, which was alternated between sets of trials at 750 or 400 Hz. During the trials the infants' heart rates were monitored to record cardiac deceleration, a reaction previously shown to correlate with the orienting reflex to a novel stimulus. While the normal infants showed the cardiac-orienting response to both onset and change of tones, the malnourished group showed no cardiac-orienting response to either condition. In addition, the normal group became habituated to repeated tones, whereas the malnourished infants evidenced inconsistent and minimal responses.

These results indicate the malnourished infants are less responsive to environmental stimuli than infants of normal weight. Thus, it is justifiable to infer that they process less information from the environment than nourished infants. Reduced responsivity or attention to impinging environmental stimulation may be a major reason why these children perform poorly on psychological tests.

(Data from West Bengal and Nepal have also shown that severely malnourished children may have a reduced responsivity to social contact; see Graves, 1976, 1978.)

The review of studies focusing on the behavioral sequelae of severe malnutrition is limited to those in which the index children were hospitalized for their nutritional condition. Studies of children with marasmus, kwashiorkor, marasmus-kwashiorkor, and undifferentiated severe malnutrition will be dealt with in order.

Marasmus

Table 9 presents a summary of the main data from three Latin American studies which were conducted on nutritionally rehabilitated marasmic children. In two of the three studies the performance of the index children on global intelligence or developmental tests was approximately one to two standard deviations below the average of 100. Unfortunately, because the ex post facto study designs furnish little premorbid data on the subjects, it is impossible to establish unequivocally the cause of intellectual impairment. Levels of maternal education, per capita income of the family, and occupation of the father are factors known to correlate with IQ score, but none of these socioeconomic factors were assessed in any of the studies reviewed. Conceivably, one or several such variables could have operated in favor of the control group.

It is noteworthy that in each of these studies marasmic children were hospitalized at an average age of less than one year. This finding is consistent with the observation of Waterlow and Rutishauser (1974) that marasmus occurs early in life, notably earlier than kwashiorkor.

Kwashiorkor

Table 10 summarizes the Latin American studies on kwashiorkor children. Examination of data from these studies yields a picture somewhat different from that of marasmic children. Evidence shows that although, in some cases, early kwashiorkor may depress intellectual functioning as measured by intelligence tests, the sequelae are not as severe as those observed in children with a history of early marasmus. Indeed, it appears that the detrimental effects of early kwashiorkor on intellectual functioning may ameliorate with time, and in some cases disappear altogether.

TABLE 9

Summary of Behavioral Studies of Children with Nutritional Marasmus

Study and Country	Experimental Subjects			Age of experimental and control Ss at evaluation	Test used and type of measure obtained	Results
	No. and description of nutritional condition	Age at time of hospital admission	No. and description of control Ss (if any)			
Brockman and Ricciuti (1971) Peru	N = 20 Diagnosed as marasmus; body weight less than 50 percent of expected for age; free of apparent edema; normal serum albumin	Mean of 10 younger children: 9.2 mo.; mean of 10 older children: 16.2 mo.	N = 19 Matched for sex and age with patients; attended regularly day care centers of Lima slums; body length at or above 10th percentile of Boston growth curves	Experimental: mean of 10 younger children: 17.9 mo.; mean of 10 older children: 34.9 mo. Controls: mean of 9 younger children: 18.7 mo.; mean of 10 older children: 33.8 mo.	Categorization behavior through 10 sorting, of 8 objects each	Average test scores: <24 mo. Exp.: 9.2 Cont.: 21.0 >24 mo. Exp.: 20.0 Cont.: 40.0
Monckeberg (1968) Chile	N = 14 Severe marasmic malnutrition	3-11 mo. (mean 6.2 mo.)		3-6 years	"Binet Method": Intelligence Quotient	Mean IQ 62; no child with IQ above 76
Pollitt (1974) Peru	N = 19 Weight deficit of 40 percent or more for age; free from edema; normal serum albumin	6-8 mo. (mean 16 mo.)	N = 28 Sibs of patients; no history of malnutrition	Experimental: 11-32 mo. (mean 22 mo.) Control: 3-30 mo. (mean 9 mo.)	Bayley Scales of mental and motor development: mental DQ; motor DQ	Results reported on mean sigma scores Mental Scale Exp.: -4.05 Cont.: -0.70 Motor Scale Exp.: -3.76 Cont.: -5.50

Source: Compiled by the author.

TABLE 10

Summary of Behavioral Studies of Children with Kwashiorkor

| Study and Country | Experimental Subjects | | No. and description of control Ss (if any) | Age of experimental and control Ss at evaluation | Test used and type of measure obtained | Results |
	No. and description of nutritional condition	Age at time hospital admission				
Barreda-Moncada (1963) Venezuela	N = 60 Growth retardation; skin change; edema; psychic changes; hair changes; liver hypertrophy	15.7–71.0 mo.		60 cases tested 7–12 wk. after hospital admission; 75 percent of cases evaluated 2 yr. later	Gesell Schedules: DQ	After 7–12 weeks of hospitalization: DQ 65 (expected 100) Marked retardation in language (DQ 50–60); most improvements in motor development (DQ 74); after 2 yr. DQ 61–88
Birch et al. (1971) Jamaica	N = 37 Edema; skin lesions; evidence of fewer dietary proteins than calories	6–30 mo.	N = 37 Healthy sibs	Experimental: 5–13 yr. Control: 5–12 yr.	Wechsler Intelligence Scale for Children: IQ	Mean IQ index: 68.5 Control: 81.5
Cavioto and Robles (1965) Mexico	N = 20 Third-degree protein-calorie malnutrition; presence of edema	6–30 mo.		1 yr. after hospitalization	Gesell Schedules: DQ	Younger (<6 mo.): Ss performance decreased with increased hospitalization Older Ss (>6 mo.): performance improved to nearly normal with hospitalization

Source: Compiled by the author.

Mixed or Severe Undifferentiated

Table 11 presents a summary of studies conducted in Mexico and Jamaica. Data from these studies are difficult to summarize because of the large variations in the children's ages at admission and testing, the degree and type of malnutrition, and the type of test used to assess intellectual functioning. The longitudinal investigation (Hertzig et al., 1972; Richardson, Birch, and Ragbeer, 1975; Richardson, 1974) in Jamaica, however, illustrates the necessity of making progressive modifications in hypotheses regarding the effects of malnutrition on intellectual functioning.

Hertzig et al. (1972), in the first paper on this project, reported findings on IQ tests given to malnourished children, their siblings, and a comparison group. The results show that IQ test scores differed among the three groups: the healthy controls scored higher than the siblings of the index group, who in turn scored higher than the malnourished children. A second paper (Richardson et al., 1973) dealt with school achievement, grades, and teacher evaluations of these same cases. The between-group differences found on these measures led to an examination of the quality of home life (Richardson, 1974) and home behavior (Richardson, Birch, and Ragbeer, 1975) of the malnourished sample. The complexity of the factors affecting the relationship between malnutrition and IQ unfolded as this study progressed, causing continual modification of the original hypothesis. The emergent network of interrelated factors surrounding the malnourished child led the investigators to suggest that the entire ecology surrounding the malnourished child must be the target of investigation, rather than the simple measurement of IQ.

One study in this section lends substantial support to this suggestion. In a longitudinal study in Mexico, Cravioto and DeLicardie (1973) and DeLicardie and Cravioto (1974) found significant differences in the quality of home life, beginning at six months of age, between children who developed malnutrition and those who did not; but they found no differences on gross measures of socioeconomic status.

Before closing this section on severe malnutrition and its effect on cognitive development, it will be useful to discuss in some detail the problems of interpreting the data that have been reviewed. The primary focus should be on the psychological tests used. The transference of tests such as the Stanford-Binet or Wechsler Scales from developed countries to rural areas or slum dwellings in Latin America for diagnostic and epidemiological purposes often assumes that normative validity of the test can be transferred. Yet this assumption has not been proven correct, and the available data suggest it is unwarranted. An analysis of the application of these tests in some of the studies reviewed shows that they have resulted in distorted

TABLE 11

Summary of Behavioral Studies Dealing with Mixed or Undifferentiated Protein-Calorie Malnutrition

Study and Country	Experimental Subjects		No. and description of control Ss (if any)	Age of experimental and control Ss at evaluation	Test used and type of measure obtained	Results
	No. and description of nutritional condition	Age at time of hospital admission				
Cravioto and DeLicardie (1973) Mexico	N = 22 Clinical kwashiorkor and marasmus (10 treated at home, 12 hospitalized)	4–53 mo.	Healthy; matched at birth for gestational age, body length, and weight	Experimental and control: birth to 58 mo.	Gesell Developmental Schedule: language development score Bipolar concept test: bipolar concept score Bettye Caldwell Inventory: home stimulation score	Index had lower language development score than controls from ca. 1 to 3 yr. Index had lower bipolar concept scores from 26 to 58 mo. Index scored lower on home stimulation score at 6 and 48 mo.
DeLicardie and Cravioto (1974) Mexico	N = 14 Subset of above children	4–38 mo.	Group CB: Subset of children in above group (ref. 21) Group CIQS: Children matched at age 5 for IQ and sex	Experimental and control: 5 yr.	Adaptation of Wechsler Preschool and Primary Scale	Index gave smaller proportion of work responses to cognitive demands than either group CB or CIQS

Reference	Index group	Age at malnutrition	Control group	Age at testing	Test	Results
Hertzig et al. (1972) Jamaica	N = 71 Diagnosed as having marasmus, kwashiorkor, or marasmic–kwashiorkor	<2 yr.	N = 71 Classmates of same sex and similar age N = 38 Health, male sibs	Experimental: 5 yr. 11 mo. to 10 yr. Sibs: 6 yr. to 12 yr. 11 mo. Control: 5 yr. to 10 yr. 11 mo.	Behavioral response to cognitive demands Wechsler Intelligence Scale for Children: IQ	Index gave fewer verbal responses than control. Mean IQ: Index 57.7 Siblings: 61.8 Control: 66.0
Richardson (1974) Jamaica	N = 71 Same children as Hertzig et al.		Control group not investigated		Home interviews with mothers or guardians: socioeconomic and environmental data	Index has poorer housing and more disadvantaged caretaker, less schooling, and higher sibling mortality
Richardson et al. (1973) Jamaica	Same index group as above except N reduced to 62		Same as above plus sib control group (N = 31)	Same as above (ref. 72)	Wide Range Achievement Test: reading, spelling, arithmetic	Index averaged 7–9 points lower on WRAT than controls; index and sibs obtain nearly identical scores

(continued)

TABLE 11 (continued)

Study and Country	Experimental Subjects		No. and description of control Ss (if any)	Age of experimental and control Ss at evaluation	Test used and type of measure obtained	Results
	No. and description of nutritional condition	Age at time of hospital admission				
					Teacher evaluation	Teacher evaluations lower for index than controls; no difference between sibs and their comparison groups
					Median school grade	Index had lower median grade than controls; no differences between sibs and their comparisons
Richardson et al. (1975) Jamaica	Same as above		Healthy: same sex sibs Classmates of same sex and similar age		Home interviews with mothers or guardians; behavioral data	Index Ss were less liked by sibs, more unhappy in school, and behaved more immaturely, clumsily, and unsocially than controls; sibs did not differ from their comparisons

Source: Compiled by the author.

data of questionable significance. For example, in the study by
Birch et al. (1971), the mean score of the index group was a statistically significant 13 points below that of the control group. The
means of both groups, however, were well below average by U.S.
standards (1.5 standard deviations below). Without an appropriate
reference group (in this case, lower-class Mexican children ranging
in age from 5 to 13 years) it is impossible to interpret the test scores
accurately and, without knowledge of the mean or standard deviation
of the population from which the reference group is drawn, no meaningful statements can be made about the levels of functioning of these
two groups.

In an attempt to cope with the problems of ex post facto design
and to control score variability due to nonnutritional factors, some
investigators have matched index and control children for demographic, social, and economic correlates of intelligence. Despite
such efforts, it is likely that the techniques of matching only account
for a few of the variables that actually differentiate malnourished
from well-nourished children. Social ecology data on severely malnourished children support the contention of nonequivalence between
index and control children in the studies reviewed. Longitudinal data
on populations in which malnutrition is endemic show that low birthweight, an indication of prenatal malnutrition, often preceded the
development of severe postnatal PEM (Stickney et al., 1976).

Moreover, many studies in Latin America (Graham and
Morales, 1963; Wray and Aguirre, 1969; Richardson, 1974) have
found that families of children with third-degree malnutrition are
more disadvantaged than the typical or average family living in the
same locale. Families of malnourished children are often more
crowded, poorer, and more unstable than families in which the children are adequately nourished. Mothers of malnourished children
were found to have less education, to be more often illiterate, and
to be in poorer health than mothers of well-nourished children. In
addition, while some studies (DeLicardie and Cravioto, 1974) have
reported no differences between control and index families on broad
indicators of socioeconomic status, significant differences on measures of maternal care were found in favor of families having adequately nourished children. It may be concluded, therefore, that
those socioeconomic and behavioral factors which distinguish between
populations with prevalent malnutrition and those without, also serve
to distinguish families with and without malnutrition within a population.

There is no way, then, of specifically determining the contribution of nonnutritional factors to the observed effects. The information as a whole strongly suggests that intellectual derangements
following severe PEM are likely to result from the synergistic effects
of nutrient deficits (including protein and energy) and conditions of
extreme poverty.

The research problems described above notwithstanding, an analysis of the studies to date provides a basis for some inferences. First, only the marasmic studies report consistent findings of detrimental effects; studies on kwashiorkor, by contrast, yield inconsistent results. Second, victims of marasmus were observed to perform about 1-2 standard deviations below control groups on mental tests; a deficit greater in magnitude than victims of other types of malnutrition. Third, marasmus, unlike other types of malnutrition, does not appear to ameliorate with age. When detrimental effects are reported with kwashiorkor, they are of relatively small magnitude and often ameliorate with age (see Pollitt and Thomson, 1977).

Observed differences in the magnitude of cognitive deficits between marasmic and kwashiorkor children may stem from the different developmental patterns of the two deficiency diseases. Nutritional marasmus is a chronic condition with an onset in early postnatal or even in prenatal life. Kwashiorkor, on the other hand, is acute and generally occurs after the first year of life. These differences in timing, both in onset and duration, may determine the severity of behavioral sequelae for two reasons: first, the onset of marasmus occurs during a period of accelerated brain growth; second, it results in a lengthy disruption of child-environment interaction that is damaging to intellectual development.

Research data have indicated that the severely malnourished child is characterized by apathy, withdrawal, low responsivity to environmental stimuli, and poor attention maintenance. This lethargic behavior ensures that the child fares poorly in competition for attention with others in the environment. As a result, learning experiences are curtailed because of reduced reciprocal mother-child interaction. Low-level functioning also limits the child's capacity to act on his own environment. Thus the low level of interaction typical of the marasmic child probably leads to developmental retardation.

Under conditions in which the nutritional deprivation is severe but of short duration, with an onset during the second year of life, the vulnerability of the child appears to be greatly reduced. In addition to the possibility of decreased vulnerability of the brain during this period, by the second year of life the child is already working with signs and symbols and, therefore, contact with the environment and learning experiences are interrupted only temporarily.

While the data currently available are insufficient to answer all the questions about intellectual impairment resulting from severe PEM, two tentative conclusions are warranted: (1) a child who suffers severe, chronic protein-energy deficiency in the first 12 months of life is likely to show severe intellectual impairment (DQ 1-2 standard deviations below average) when compared with standards for his population; (2) a child suffering severe, acute protein-energy deficiency in the second year of life is not likely to show intellectual impairment (as measured by developmental tests) when compared with standards for his population (see Pollitt and Thomson, 1977, for a more detailed discussion of these conclusions).

MILD-TO-MODERATE PEM

Except for the quasi-experimental studies discussed in the next chapter, the work on mild-to-moderate malnutrition is limited compared to the work on severe protein-energy malnutrition. Table 12 presents in summary form the main data from three published correlational studies conducted in Latin America on the effects of mild-to-moderate malnutrition.

The three studies included in the table were based on ex post facto study design and as such are susceptible to the same criticisms previously presented in connection with severe PEM. In addition, while the diagnosis of severe PEM is based on clinical signs, the diagnoses of mild-to-moderate malnutrition in the studies listed were based on anthropometric data, an indirect measure. Although this is a standard procedure in nutrition surveys and nutrition epidemiology, it does not meet acceptable scientific standards for the measurements of a variable in behavioral research. This is so because while nutrition is a potent determinant of physical growth, it is not the only factor that affects body size. Genetic factors, hormonal regulation and timing, and other environmental factors also have significant effects on growth (for example, see Pollitt and Ricciuti, 1969).

All three studies found a significant positive covariation among anthropometric measures and behavioral test scores. These findings are particularly meaningful because the three projects focused on children of different age ranges, and used behavioral measures that probably tapped different cognitive dimensions. All three studies, however, also found that significant test score variations could be explained in terms of selected socioenvironmental variables such as maternal education or family income. Indeed, in two of the three studies (Klein et al., 1972; Pollitt, 1973) it was impossible to separate the variance attributed to the anthropometry variables from that attributed to the socioenvironmental factors.

From the data reviewed it seems fair to conclude that among populations in which malnutrition is endemic, infants and young children of comparatively low stature are likely to perform less well on aggregate tests of intelligence or on tests of specific cognitive processes (for example, language or perception) than are average

TABLE 12

Summary of Behavioral Studies Dealing with Mixed or Moderate Protein-Energy Malnutrition

Study and Country	No. and description of samples		Age of Children	Tests Used	Results
	Experimental	Control			
Cravioto et al. (1966) Guatemala	(Total of 143 rural children) Rural: lower quartile for height distribution	Rural: upper quartile for height distribution Urban: 120 children from private school; upper middle or upper SES	6 to 11 years old	Intersensory integration tasks	Significant difference in performance in tests of intersensory integration between samples. Shorter children performed worse.
Klein et al. (1977) Guatemala	172 children from 4 rural villages where PEM is endemic Nutritional status defined by anthropometric measurements		3 to 6 years old	1. Language facility 2. Short-term memory for numbers 3. Perceptual analysis 4. Socioeconomic data also collected	Anthropometric and socioeconomic variables accounted for modest amount of variance, primarily in memory and perceptual test.
Pollitt (1972) Peru	39 children from urban slums in Lima were divided into 4 groups by height and socioeconomic status (2 × 2 design)		6 to 53 months old	Sorting and manipulative tasks	The only group that differed significantly was short-lowest socioeconomic group.

Source: Compiled by the author.

size children from the same community. It is also evident that among these populations infants and young children of comparatively small stature are more likely to come from families in the lowest socioeconomic stratum than are children of similar age but average size.

IODINE DEFICIENCY

Iodine is not distributed evenly over the earth's crust. In any geographic location soil contains more iodine than rock because of iodine retention by plants and absorption of iodine from sources such as sea mist. Consequently, marked deficiencies occur in most of the mountainous areas of the world. It is not surprising, therefore, that iodine deficiency is highly prevalent in Andean populations and represents a significant public health problem in Latin America. The problem extends from the highlands of Mexico and Central America, through the Andean chain, and as far south as Chile and Argentina (Organizacion Panamericana de la Salud, 1976).

Severe iodine deficiency results in hypothyroidism, a pathological state characterized by an impairment of the ability to synthesize thyroid hormones. Unless the thyroid gland is nonfunctional or absent, this impairment is accompanied by goiter, or thyroid gland enlargement, which results from hyperstimulation of the thyroid gland to secrete thyroid hormones. Endemic goiter has been associated with a mean daily estimated iodine intake of less than 40-50 Hg. Endemic in this case refers to localization of this condition within a specific geographic area (Matovinovic et al., 1974; Stanbury, 1977). It is important to note, however, that prevalence and incidence of endemic cretinism covaries with the socioeconomic conditions of the community (Fierro-Benitez et al., 1969). The interactions between social factors, iodine deficiency, and genetic predispositions remain unknown (Stanbury, 1972).

It has been difficult to establish reliable measures for the prevalence of endemic goiter in South America because there are wide variations among different communities which are relatively close to one another. Moreover, prevalence rates change significantly over relatively short periods of time following iodine prophylaxis programs. For example, from 1950 to 1960 the prevalence of goiter among 5- to 19-year-old subjects in three towns in the Cauca Valley in Colombia dropped from nearly 100 percent to approximately 20 percent (OPS, 1976).

Table 13 presents some prevalence figures for endemic goiter in several South American countries over various years. The data are relatively old and, given the operation of several new

TABLE 13

Prevalence of Endemic Goiter in South America

Country	Prevalence		
	10 Percent	10–19 Percent	20–29 Percent
Argentina (1968)		12–50	
Bolivia (1970)		15–66	
Brazil (1970–1972)		11–59	
Colombia (1965)	x		
Chile (1964–1967)	x		
Ecuador (1970)		12–28	
Panama (1967)[a]		x	
Paraguay (1973–1974)[a]		x	
Peru (1967)			x
Uruguay (1965)			x
Venezuela (1966)		x	

x: Indicates range of prevalence rates.
[a] De Maeyer, E. M., Lowenstein, F. W., Tailly, C. H., La Lucha Contra el Bocio Endemico, Organizacion Mundial de la Salud, Geneva, Switzerland, 1979.
Source: PAHO, 1974b.

prophylactic programs, are likely to have changed during the recent past. Nonetheless, they point out the magnitude of the problem and suggest that a significant portion of the South American population continues to be affected by a condition which is subject to easy eradication.

Severe endemic goiter has been clearly associated with endemic cretinism in different regions of the world. In Latin America this association was well-established even among pre-Colombian Indians (Rueda-Williamson, 1974). A "cretin" is characterized by severe intellectual retardation, short stature, dysarthria, and possibly deafness (PAHO, 1974; Delange et al., 1972; Dodge et al., 1969; Dunn, 1972). A differentiation has been made between the neurological form of cretinism and the myxedematous form. The former is primarily characterized by deaf-mutism and spastic-like movements. In the myxedematous form, physical growth is more significantly affected but deaf-mutism is absent and the clinical signs are concordant with clinical hypothyroidism (Stanbury, 1977).

A continuum of neurological impairment resulting from iodine deficiency has been postulated. The end points of the continuum represent cretinism and milder neurological impairment, respectively (Fierro-Benitez et al., 1974). Although little argument exists about the association between goiter, severe mental retardation, and cretinism, there is still considerable doubt about the continuum hypothesis. Specifically, the existence of milder forms of cognitive deficits associated with iodine deficiency has not been conclusively demonstrated. The significance of this hypothesis should be obvious. If it is correct, then it is legitimate to infer that iodine deficiency has resulted in the neurological impairment of a sizable number of children on the continent.

L. S. Greene (1977), in a study in La Esperanza, an Andean community in Ecuador, provides some support for the hypothesis that among so-called normal individuals in an area afflicted with endemic cretinism there is a relatively high prevalence of physical and/or neurological deficit. For this purpose he utilized the Bender-Gestalt test, which measures the maturation of visual motor perception. This test consists of a series of nine figures, which the subjects observe and are asked to reproduce. The test is evaluated by measuring the number of errors made in reproduction. The subjects, natives of La Esperanza, included 344 normal individuals and 45 deaf-mutes, ranging in age from 15 to 54 years. The results indicated that in addition to the severe deficit displayed by the deaf-mutes, 17.4 percent of the normal population (24 percent of the females and 7.3 percent of the males) exhibited some degree of neurological deficit.

Evidence accumulated from studies on the effects of iodized oil on pregnant women also provides some support for the continuum hypothesis. Moreover, these data suggest that the adverse effects of iodine deficiency on the central nervous system begin during early stages of fetal life. Fierro-Benitez and colleagues (1974) in Ecuador compared the IQs of children from two communities exposed to different iodine treatments. In one, Tocachi, iodized oil was injected into every member of the community; the other community served as a control. Children in Tocachi were selected for the study if they were at least 36 months old and if treatment of their mothers had occurred either prior to conception or between the fourth and fifth month of fetal life. They were then matched by age and sex with children from La Esperanza. The Stanford-Binet mean IQ for the children of the mothers treated during gestation was 71.7 (s.d. = 14.6), and for their controls it was 69.6 (s.d. = 13.3); this difference was statistically nonsignificant. On the other hand, the mean IQ for the offsprings of the women treated prior to conception was 83.6 (s.d. = 13.4) and for the controls it was 72.7 (s.d. = 14); this difference was highly significant ($p < .002$). It follows that treatment has a differential effect over intelligence as a function of the timing of implementation. Treatment initiated during the second trimester of pregnancy does not appear to have a preventive effect over (possible) mild intellectual retardation associated with iodine deficiency. Conversely, it does have a potent salutary effect if it is implemented prior to embryogenesis.

In summary, it should be apparent that, despite the existence of a few pioneering studies, there is much work to be done in this area. There is little, if any, information on the possible interactive effects of iodine deficiency and protein-energy malnutrition on the central nervous system function of children. It seems likely that many of the deficiencies attributed to subjects selected from communities where goiter is endemic could be the result of other nutritional deficiencies. Moreover, little is known about the social and cultural factors that contribute to the prevalence of goiter and associated mental retardation. Finally, the tests that have been used are culturally inappropriate for the subjects tested and are of questionable diagnostic specificity given the initial questions posed. It is unlikely, for example, that accurate discriminations could be made between culturally bound graphic deficiencies and neurologically determined errors in the Bender test used by Greene (1977). This is an area which needs further exploration.

IRON DEFICIENCY

Prevalence statistics on iron deficiency without anemia are not yet available from large-scale epidemiological studies in South America, but it may be expected that in many communities 50 percent or more of the population would be iron deficient. In spite of the magnitude of the iron deficiency problem on the continent, no published information is yet available on its functional consequences among children. Most of the data in this area come from studies conducted in the United States, where the size of the problem is also reason for public health concern. Inconclusive information suggests that particular process features of cognition such as selective attention, attention maintenance, or necessary rehearsal strategies may be impaired by iron deficiency (for a review of literature, see Leibel, Greenfield, and Pollitt, 1979). These impairments do not appear to depend on deficits in tissue oxygenation associated with hematological changes, but are likely to be dependent on iron-mediated alterations in brain biochemistry (see Oski and Honig, 1978; Pollitt, Greenfield and Leibel, 1978). Thus, even mild forms of iron deficiency (without anemia) may have some adverse effects in cognitive operations.

If the data reported in the United States are conclusively validated, the implications are serious for those Latin American countries with large populations of vulnerable children. In the light of such evidence, and in the Latin American context, it becomes extremely important to determine whether or not functional alterations resulting from iron deficiency interact with the general nutritional status of the child. These alterations may be especially serious when they occur in a child whose nutritional status also presents a protein-energy deficit.

CONCLUSION

The high prevalence of PEM, and iodine and iron deficiency are major public health concerns in Latin America. Moreover, in terms of the functional consequences discussed in this chapter, it is of particular importance to note that these nutritional deficiencies go hand-in-hand with poverty. Malnutrition is primarily a condition of the poor and, as noted in Chapter 2, poverty is an obstacle to the cognitive and educational development of children. A child who is both poor and malnourished, then, is in double jeopardy. His chances of adapting successfully to an industrialized, technologically oriented society are seriously limited.

From the data reviewed in this chapter it is clear that, while much remains to be learned, there exists a significant body of knowledge dealing with the relationship between malnutrition and mental development. Moreover, this knowledge is solid enough to be used effectively in establishing priorities and guidelines for public health action. In summary, the following conclusions can be drawn: (1) long-term severe PEM during the first year of life is likely to result in serious deficits in cognitive function; (2) among communities where PEM malnutrition is endemic, comparatively undersized-underweight children will exhibit a poorer performance on tests of intellectual function than will children of average size from the same community; (3) among communities where malnutrition is endemic, signs of severe malnutrition in a child are generally an indication of social and economic stress in the family of the child; (4) in communities where there is iodine deficiency and endemic goiter, there is a greater prevalence of endemic cretinism and different derangements of mental function than in other communities of similar economic development but without iodine deficiency; and (5) eradication of endemic goiter through effective prophylactic intervention programs results in a significant drop in the prevalence of cretinism and mental retardation.

4
INTERVENTION PROGRAMS: QUASI-EXPERIMENTAL STUDIES

The previous chapter presented a discussion of the ways in which cognitive development is affected by poverty in general and malnutrition in particular. Those effects are discussed in this chapter in connection with four experimental intervention programs that have operated in Latin America within the past ten years. All the programs shared the objective of generating research data on the effects of PEM on behavior. They also have in common the researchers' manipulation of part of the dietary intake of the participants and their interest in the covariations between physical growth and mental development.

The children selected for treatment in these experimental studies were either malnourished or at risk of malnutrition. This was an important entry criterion because the existence of a causal relationship between malnutrition and developmental retardation was treated as a working hypothesis. In order to control for covariate effects, most of these studies also investigated the relationships among the experimental and outcome variables and their associated socioeconomic factors (for example, parental education, family income). Two of the programs (Klein et al., 1977; Chavez and Martinez, 1979) restricted their intervention to dietary supplementation, while the remaining two (Mora et al., 1979; McKay et al., 1978) added a psychoeducational intervention to their experimental protocol.

Table 14 outlines substantive characteristics of the four studies. They are labeled quasi-experimental following Campbell and Stanley (1973) terminology: the investigators have some control over timing and degree of nutritional status variance, but there is no control over other important and recognized conditions that determine the effectiveness of the experimental variable. The following is a detailed discussion of the strengths and weaknesses of the quasi-experimental design in these particular cases.

TABLE 14

Brief Outline of Intervention Programs

Investigator and Community	Developmental Period	Nature of Nutrition Intervention	Delivery System	Nature of Psychological Stimulation	Data on Outcome Variable Available
Chavez, A., et al. One small village, Mexico (1978)	Began 6th week of pregnancy, first 5 years of life	Iron, vitamins, powdered milk	Daily feeding station	None controlled	Mother-infant interaction—Gesell
Klein, R., et al. 4 Indian villages, Guatemala (1977)	Began 3rd month of pregnancy; first 6 years of life	1) 1 8-oz. cup Atole: 163 Kcal; 11 gm. protein 2) 1 8-oz. cup Fresco: 59 Kcal	Daily feeding station	None controlled	Battery of psychological tests developed at INCAP
McKay, H., et al. Urban slum, Cali, Colombia (1978)	3rd–6th year of life	70–80% of RDA protein and calories, 100 percent of vitamins and minerals	At day care centers	Day care center	Large battery of tests
Mora, J. O., et al. Urban slum, Bogota, Colombia (1978)	Began 6th month of pregnancy, first 4 years of life	623 Kcal, 30 gm. protein daily; except pregnant women: 856 Kcal, 38 gm. protein	Every other work day	Intrafamily household stimulation	Griffith Scale, INCAP battery and others

Source: Compiled by the author.

A major strength of the quasi-experimental approach has been the relative control over the subject's dietary intake and, therefore, over nutritional status variance. The probability of detecting covariations between nutritional status and cognitive development is significantly greater in these studies than in correlation studies. This experimental control permitted the advancement of refined hypotheses regarding the nature of the nutrition-behavior linkage. In addition, the joint use of nutrition and psychoeducational interventions in two studies made feasible the assessment of interaction between biological and social variables. The study of this interaction is crucially important for understanding the effects of nutrition on behavior.

It should be noted, however, that attempts to monitor total dietary intake (food supplement plus home diet) were difficult if not impossible. Investigators were forced to make gross estimates of the extent to which the nutrition treatment replaced, rather than supplemented, the regular diet of the recipients (see Mora et al., 1978). In addition, a lack of specificity made it difficult to establish accurately which components of the diet (for example, calories or protein) were responsible for detected effects.

A similar problem exists with regard to psychoeducational intervention; that is, investigators have been unable to define precisely the nature of the intervention (for detailed discussion of these issues see Pollitt and Thomson, 1977). Operational definitions of the treatments have often excluded important elements of the treatment variable or have failed to establish their independent or interactive effects on the outcome measures (see McKay et al., 1978). Other cases provide little in the way of either documentation or conceptualization regarding the exact nature of the treatment (see Christensen et al., 1977a and b).

In addition, both nutrition and psychoeducational interventions have exhibited a lack of regard for the possibility of treatment-context interaction (Chavez and Martinez, 1979). That is, treatment may have activated the behavior which produced, in turn, the type of effects attributed to the treatment. This issue emphasizes the lack of theory in two important areas in these studies: (1) malnutrition-causality at the family and community level, and (2) the impact of social factors on mental development. As a result, a theory-free approach is commonly used in selecting those environmental variables which, in conjunction with treatment variables, are presumed to shape the development of the child. Consequently, there has been little consensus among investigators as to which variables should be investigated, measured, and controlled.

NEWBORN AND NEONATAL PERIOD

Birth weight data are discussed in this chapter because of the association between low birth weight and subsequent behavioral and cognitive derangements (Hunt, 1976). If the use of nutrition supplementation in a given population reduces the prevalence of low birth weight babies and increases the mean birth weight, it can be assumed that the prevalence of cognitive derangements will also be decreased.

Nutritional supplementation during the prenatal period has face validity; however, the available data from the quasi-experimental studies on this particular issue are not conclusive. The data from the longitudinal study of INCAP in four rural villages in Guatemala (Klein et al., 1977) concentrated on the contribution of supplemental calories to total nutrient intake during pregnancy, and on the relationship between birth weight and food supplementation during pregnancy. The supplements were delivered in a feeding station on a daily schedule. They began in the first trimester and continued through the seventh year of postnatal life in the offspring of these women. When all subjects participating in the study were aggregated, a small but statistically significant correlation (.135) was found between birth weight of the offspring and calorie supplementation during pregnancy (Lechtig et al., 1975). On the basis of this coefficient, it can be estimated that only about 2 percent ($r^2 = .018$) of the birth weight variance could be attributed to the supplementation program.

A statistical comparison was also made between the birth weights of the offsprings of two groups of pregnant women with different levels of calorie supplementation. As expected, the birth weight of the offsprings of women with a total supplementation intake above 20,000 calories was significantly higher than that of women with an intake below 20,000 calories. The mean birth weight for high-calorie-intake babies was 3,105 grams versus 2,994 grams for the low-calorie infants. Approximately 17 percent of the supplemented but low-calorie group and 8 percent of the high-calorie group were low birth weight babies ($\leq 2,500$ grams).

The degree of variance in birth weight ($r^2 = .02$) which is accounted for by nutritional intervention is of questionable biological significance. From a public health perspective, one which is concerned with populations, focusing on the effects of supplementation on mean birth weight is not encouraged. On the other hand, reduction of 50 percent in the prevalence of low birth weight babies may be meaningful. This reduction, however, was limited to a subset of the participants. The prevalence of low birth weight among low-calorie recipients of the program was 17 percent. This percentage is relatively high (see Puffer and Serrano, 1973) and there is no way of determining whether this prevalence differs from nonsupplemented groups in the villages in question. Accordingly, the study indicates that high intake of calories, rather than the supplemental program as a whole, has beneficial effects.

The study in Bogota, Colombia (Mora et al., 1979) also compared the growth of newborns, infants, and children with and without supplementation and included a psychoeducational component. The supplementation program in this study, however, differs somewhat from that of INCAP in both timing and method of delivery. Supplementation in the INCAP study was initiated in the first trimester of pregnancy, but in Colombia the treatment began in the last trimester. Moreover, in contrast to INCAP, where the daily supplement was delivered in a feeding station, the supplementation in this study was delivered weekly in a field unit similar to a neighborhood store. The supplement package was an amount of food that made feasible adequate distribution among all family members. It was estimated that the pregnant woman would receive enough supplement to meet a substantial proportion of the recommended dietary allowances for a subject of her physiological status.

In Colombia the mean birth weight of the offsprings of unsupplemented control women was 2,932 grams, and for the supplemented group it was 2,992. This 60-gram difference was statistically significant, but an analysis of the data by sex showed that while supplementation has a significant effect on males (supplemented = 3,061 grams; unsupplemented = 2,947 grams) there was no effect on females (supplemented = 2,947; unsupplemented = 2,935 grams). Likewise, when the proportion of low birth weight babies was determined for the total sample and by sex, it was found that only among supplemented males was there any statistically meaningful drop in occurrence of low birth weight in comparison with the unsupplemented sample (supplemented males = 5.6 percent; unsupplemented males = 14.6 percent). Here again, the results are not encouraging from a public health perspective, even if it is assumed that a gain of 100 grams among male infants is biologically significant. The beneficiaries are males, or only about one-half of the recipients; epidemiologically it is presently impossible to predict the sex of the fetus.

The investigators in both Guatemala and Bogota tried to determine the extent to which the nutritional supplement represented a true supplement as opposed to a substitution for the mother's daily diet. The information collected from 24-hour records suggests that in the Bogota sample there was an increment of both calories and protein over the regular diet, but that in the Guatemala sample the increment was limited to calories. Neither study documents conclusively the extent to which the total intake (supplement plus home diet) met the physiological requirements of a pregnant mother.

It is conceivable that nutritional supplementation may affect early postnatal behavior without producing a detectable effect on somatic growth. This hypothesis is partly supported by some recent data from the Bogota study. Using gaze time at a checker board as a measure of attention, the investigators found that at 15 days of age the supplemented group, on the average, habituated faster and gazed longer at the figure than did the unsupplemented controls. In contrast to the birth weight data, however, an analysis by sex of the habituation rate in both groups showed treatment effects on females, but not on males (Vuori et al., 1979). No published data on the effects of psychoeducational intervention on neonatal behavior are yet available for these studies.

INFANCY (1-24 MONTHS)

In the first year of life and part of the second, cognitive function is based primarily on neuromotor function, sensorimotor responsiveness, and perceptual alertness. Receptive and expressive language become salient components of cognition in the latter part of the first year, and gradually develop into the axis of symbolic function. In light of these developmental considerations, it seems justified to assume that prenatal history, nutritional status, and physical health will be major influences on cognitive development during the first two years of life. Conversely, learning experiences, especially those which emphasize language, may not exert potent influence over cognitive growth until the child enters the second or third year of life. Given these considerations, it is possible to analyze the available data on the effects of nutrition supplementation and psychoeducational intervention on mental development.

Results from the INCAP studies investigating the effects of pre- and postnatal food supplementation on developmental scales have been published by Klein and collaborators (1977). By 15 months of age statistically significant correlations appear between level of supplementation and scores on the Guatemalan mental and motor scales; .130 and .134, respectively. Although both coefficients are small, they are statistically significant ($p < .05$) by reason of the sample size, 460 subjects. By 24 months the same correlational analysis yielded coefficients of .16 and .22. Following an item analysis of the scales, the data showed that the treatment appeared to have been more closely associated with motor and manipulative aptitude items than with other early components of cognitive function. This observation is in keeping with the developmental propositions advanced previously.

By 36 months of age there were statistically meaningful correlations between the level of supplementation and both vocabulary development and verbal inferences. It is important to note, however, that the coefficients were again approximately .15 and none of them was above .20. As already indicated, these levels of association achieve statistical significance because of the large sample size. Even using the largest of the coefficients to ascertain the effects of treatment accounts for only 2 to 3 percent of the variance in the outcome variable.

Statistical findings such as those reported from the INCAP study are not unequivocal and, therefore, may be interpreted according to conceptual perspective or professional interest. In analyzing the INCAP findings regarding cause-effect relationship, it is necessary to focus on both the statistical significance and magnitude of the coefficients.

When a given regression coefficient reaches an accepted level of statistical significance (that is, $< .01$), it is the magnitude and not the level of significance which establishes the degree of causal relationship between variables. For example, in two similar studies looking at the effects of two different drugs on the same behavior, different sample sizes are used: namely, 35 and 350 subjects. Following data analysis, it is found that in the study with the smallest sample (35), the coefficient of correlation between the experimental treatment and the outcome variables is .65, with $p = .01$. In the study with a sample of 350, the same bivariate correlation is .30, with $p = .001$. Accordingly, it may be inferred that the drug in the study with 35 subjects is more effective, as it accounted for more of the variability in the behavior in question than did the alternate. Indeed, the former and latter drugs account for 42 percent and 9 percent, respectively, of the variance in the same outcome variable.

Although many of the correlation coefficients reported by the INCAP group may be statistically meaningful, it does not follow necessarily that they describe biologically meaningful events. Most of the coefficients of correlation are small ($\cong .20$) and the variance they explain is almost negligible. It is the author's impression that few of the correlations reported by Klein and collaborators could stand the close scrutiny of an analyst interested in significance from a biological, rather than a statistical, perspective.

Chavez and Martinez (1979) conducted a longitudinal study in Mexico that attempted to "seek to prove definitely the hypothesis that an improvement in the nutritional status in a group of children, even without modifying the environment, causes positive change in their physical and mental development and also in their behavior." They used a between-group comparison research design: one group exposed to a nutrition supplementation program and the other group used as control. Neither group had more than 20 subjects. Supplementation began at approximately 45 days of pregnancy and continued to about 4 years of age. Supplementation of children was initiated when maternal milk became inadequate for physiological growth requirements. The study was conducted in a relatively stable, small, low-income, rural community, geographically distant from any large urban center, where feeding practices were characterized by prolonged breast-feeding and late introduction of solids.

By the 24th week of age a number of important behavioral differences were observed between groups. In comparison to the non-supplemented group, the experimental children slept less during the day, spent less time in the cradle, spent more time in "free play," and maintained more frequent contact with their siblings. After about the sixth month of life, there were also large differences in mother-child interaction. The supplemented group, in comparison to the controls, maintained more independent behavior. The authors report that "at one year of age, the supplemented child was three times more active, and at two years of age as much as six times more active than the nonsupplemented group." It was apparent that the growth and development of both groups of children were different in many ways; physically, socially, emotionally, and cognitively, the supplemented group was much more advanced and mature than the nonsupplemented group. In this study, the large statistical differences between groups clearly expressed the large developmental differences between index and control children who had been exposed to different life experiences.

The data on the developmental course of the index and contrast children are conclusive evidence of the plasticity of the human organism during early periods of life. Chavez and Martinez have shown that the growth and development of rural, poor infants at risk of malnutrition can be protected, and that with adequate manipulations of environmental contingencies, gains can be made in their growth velocity. It is the impression of the author, however, that they have failed in their attempt to "prove definitely" that an improvement in the nutritional conditions (without modifying other environmental conditions) causes positive changes in the physical and mental development of the target children. It is necessary to recognize that the delivery of the supplements for both mothers and infants in the index group was made in a research station within this small rural community. Twice a day the 17 experimental dyads attended the station where, in addition to receiving the nutrition supplements, they also had the opportunity of establishing contact with the experimenters and with other participants of the program. Thus, strictly speaking, the intervention was not restricted to nutrition, but also included the social sphere. Moreover, participation in the program was likely to have a "prestige" component within the rural community, and it is difficult to identify the ways in which such an aura affected the caretaking behavior of the parents in the experimental group. This is not to deny that the nutrition intervention explains a significant part of the developmental changes in the index children, but to recognize that other factors in the intervention were as significant, if not more so, as the nutrition delivery program.

PRESCHOOL PERIOD (3-6 YEARS)

In Chapter 2 reference was made to the study conducted by McKay et al. (1978) in Cali, Colombia. The focus was then restricted to the data on the cognitive development of children prior to exposure to the intervention program. In this section the focus is shifted and primary attention is given to the beneficial effects of the day care experience. The intervention program included educational activities, nutrition supplementation, and medical care.

Entry requirements included height and weight measurements indicating mild-to-moderate malnutrition at the time the study was initiated. All cases were selected from neighborhoods in Cali which were noted for their extreme poverty. The study design called for four different treatment periods, each of a different duration and each beginning at a different time period in the development of the children. The first and longest treatment began when the children were about 42 months old; the last and shortest treatment began when the mean age of the respective group was about 74 months. Two control groups were used in the study; one from the same low-income group from which the treated samples were selected, the other from a high socioeconomic group in the city of Cali.

As described by the investigators, an average treatment day consisted of six hours of integrated health, nutritional, and educational activities, in which approximately four hours were devoted to education and two hours to health, nutrition, and hygiene. In practice, the nutrition and health care program provided opportunities to reinforce many aspects of the education curriculum, and time in the education program was used to reinforce recommended hygiene and food consumption practices.

Behavioral testing was conducted before and after treatment periods. Variations in the types of tests used for different ages assured that the tests were appropriate for each of the developmental stages under study. In most instances, however, the tests measured different aspects of receptive and expressive language, memory, manual dexterity and motor control, concept formation, and logical

TABLE 15

Scaled Scores on General Cognitive Ability, Means and
Estimated Standard Errors, of the Four Treatment
Groups and Group HS at Five Testing Points

Group	N	Average Age at Testing (months)				
		43	49	63	77	87
		Mean score				
HS	28	- .11	.39	2.28	4.27	4.89
T4	50	-1.82[a]	.21	1.80	3.35	3.66
T3	47	-1.72	-1.06	1.64	3.06	3.35
T2	49	-1.94	-1.22	.30[b]	2.61	3.15
T1	90	1.83	-1.11	.33	2.07	2.73
		Estimated standard error				
HS	28	.192	.196	.166	.191	.198
T4	50	.225	.148	.138	.164	.152
T3	47	.161	.136	.103	.123	.120
T2	49	.131	.132	.115	.133	.125
T1	90	.110	.097	.098	.124	.108
		Standard deviation				
All Groups		1.161	1.153	1.169	1.263	1.164

[a] Calculated from 42 percent sample tested prior to beginning
of treatment.

[b] Calculated from 50 percent sample tested prior to beginning
of treatment.

Source: McKay et al., Science 1978.

50

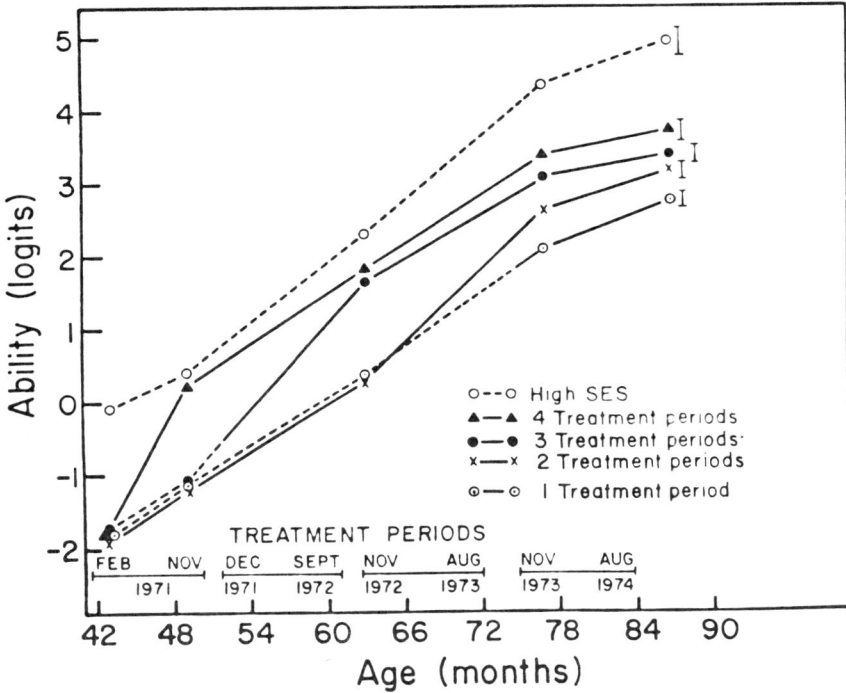

FIGURE 1

Growth of General Cognitive Ability

Note: Growth of general cognitive ability of the children from age 43 months to 87 months, the age at the beginning of primary school. Ability scores are scaled sums of test items correct among items common to proximate testing points. The solid lines represent periods of participation in a treatment sequence, and brackets to the right of the curves indicate ±1 standard error of the corresponding group means at the fifth measurement point. At the fourth measurement point there are no overlapping standard errors; at earlier measurement points there is overlap only among obviously adjacent groups.

Source: McKay et al., Science 1978.

thinking. Although the response vectors were not the same at the different test periods, a principal component analysis showed that one underlying factor explained most of the test score variance at each evaluation period. On the basis of this apparent unidimensionality of cognitive function, the investigators used an aggregate score (described as general cognitive ability) for all within- and between-group comparisons.

The scaled scores on "general cognitive ability" for the various groups (except for the nontreated low-income sample) are included in Table 15. Moreover, the growth of general cognitive ability for each of these groups is also presented in Figure 1.

Both the table and the figure clearly illustrate that by 87 months of age the group with the longest treatment has the highest performance among the treated samples. Another important finding is that for all four groups the slope of the curves immediately after the initiation of the treatment will vary as a function of the age of the children. That is, the younger the child, the greater the initial impact of the treatment. It is also important to note that, among those who commenced treatment at 42 and 54 months, there is a tendency over time to lose some of the initial gain. Finally, it should be noted that, despite the significant impact of the treatments, none of the children reached the level of performance of the high-income children.

By the time the children were eight years old, or one year after termination of the study, the treated group still exhibited differences in cognitive function in the expected direction. Thus, effects appear to have been maintained even in the absence of continued treatment. These data, however, should not be interpreted to mean that such differences will persist throughout the entire developmental period. Data on compensatory preschool programs in the United States indicate that differences may disappear over time (Bronfenbrenner, 1974).

An important question remains concerning whether or not the differences in cognitive ability between the high-income sample and the experimental group with the longest treatment period would have disappeared had the treatment been initiated before the children were 42 months old. This query is important if the aim is to equalize the intellectual competence of the low-income children and that of the economically advantaged groups of society.

CONCLUSIONS

The four quasi-experimental studies reviewed were born from academic concerns regarding the effects of PEM on behavioral development. Recognition of the methodological deficiencies and limitations inherent in past correlation studies led the investigators to manipulate dietary intake and psychoeducational inputs. While their approach represented a step forward in the field, other methodological and conceptual problems pervade these studies and cloud the interpretation of the findings. Salient among these problems are: (1) the extent to which the experimental diet substitutes for the home diet; (2) a lack of specificity on the nature of the psychoeducational inputs; and (3) definition of treatment-context interactions. All four studies give evidence of the plasticity of the human organism and its vulnerability to adverse environmental circumstances during early developmental periods. More importantly, perhaps, from an applied perspective they have shown that some of the deficits in intellectual functions that accompany poverty and malnutrition can be prevented or ameliorated through improved diet, learning experiences, and health surveillance. In contrast to previous assumptions, the data from some of these studies show that even after the third year of life a marked improvement in life conditions will result in major performance gains on tests of cognitive function. The evidence also indicates that interventions restricted to nutrition supplementation do not have major impact on the cognitive development of the recipients. The correlations that have been reported among levels of supplementation and behavioral test performance may be statistically meaningful, but they are numerically small and of questionable biological significance.

5
COMMUNITY INTERVENTION PROGRAMS

A number of community intervention programs developed in Latin America aim at the prevention of cognitive deficits associated with poverty and malnutrition. There is a substantive difference, however, between these programs and the quasi-experimental programs described in the previous chapter. The latter attempted to clarify the nature of the effects of adverse biosocial environments in general and malnutrition in particular on mental development. They were each initiated (except for the study by Chavez et al., 1979) by people working in institutions outside the country in which the study took place and, while they were not totally detached from applied considerations, at the outset their primary concerns were academic. On the other hand, the community projects focused on applied goals, their research objectives were restricted to evaluation of the effectiveness of their intervention strategy, and those responsible were natives of the countries in which the studies were conducted.

This chapter presents descriptions of selected community programs for infants and preschool children that have operated or are operating in Chile, Colombia, and Peru, and for which documentation is available. (Community intervention programs in Venezuela are described in Chapter 8.) Evaluation data from these studies are not as detailed and methodologically sound as those from the quasi-experimental studies, but they do provide additional information on intervention strategies used with economically impoverished children, and aid in clarifying which modes of operation are most likely to be successful.

The main goal of the community programs described is to prevent cognitive defects, but there are significant differences among them in terms of educational philosophy and conceptions of the developmental needs of low-income children. There are also differences in sponsorship. Some projects are private efforts organized and implemented by concerned, socially committed professionals; others are publicly funded programs, some of which may be initiated as pilot projects before a major operation begins.

CHILE

Program of Early Stimulation

The pilot program was implemented by the professional staff of the National Health Service of Chile, Mental Health Section (Montenegro et al., 1977). It analyzed the effects of a home-based program in early stimulation on the psychosocial development of infants from 0 to two years of age whose mothers had participated in the program. The program also attempted to: (1) improve maternal effectiveness in caretaking; (2) demonstrate that an effective intervention program can be based on the available infrastructure of the National Health Service; and (3) propose an intervention procedure suitable for large-scale operations.

Implicit in this approach is the philosophy that cognitive deficits associated with poverty stem from intrafamily conditions and parental behaviors that operate as obstacles to infant development. Appropriate modification of such conditions and behaviors would result in a developmental course in keeping with an infant's potential. It is also assumed that exposure of mothers to paraprofessional personnel and selected educational material can bring about major behavioral changes.

Twenty-four stimulation manuals (Lira and Folch, 1978, 1978a) were prepared for use by mothers; one per month for the first two years of life. Each included several pages of instructions and demonstrations on caretaking; descriptions of situations which allegedly would stimulate the child's coordination and motor, language, and social development; and instructions for caretaking norms that "would enhance an adequate relationship between parents and children and the formation of habits in the children" (p. 9). The investigators encouraged the use of situations that would develop naturally within the household, or that could be incorporated into the general daily routine.

For the purposes of evaluation, mothers in treatment and control groups were chosen at random from among pregnant, low-income women visiting National Health Service outpatient clinics for prenatal examinations. One objective of the evaluation was to maintain a group of children who were representative of the population attending the centers serviced by the National Health Service. Mothers of premature children and those who had experienced complications during pregnancy or delivery were excluded from sampling.

Five study groups were set up. GE1 included 42 infants exposed do the stimulation curriculum for the first 24 months of life. GE2 included 12 subjects who were exposed to the stimulation curriculum from the fourth to the twenty-fourth month of life and who were evaluated once a month. GE3 was made up of 40 control infants whose exposure to the curriculum did not begin until approximately the 14th month. Mothers of these infants received visits from auxiliary personnel up to the 13th month; for control purposes, however, these visits were restricted to discussion of the physical growth of the children. GC1 was a control group without treatment, evaluated every three months. GC2 was a control group of middle to high income families.

In order to understand the findings of this study more fully, it is pertinent to describe in some detail the nature of the experimental intervention. Prior to the birth of the index children in GE1 the investigators met with participating parents to explain the project. Each mother was then visited at home and given a copy of the Manual for the Newborn. Weekly visits were initiated after delivery, each lasting about 30 minutes and following the format described in the manual. At the end of the first month the mothers attended one of four outpatient departments and the first psychomotor assessment of the participating infants was conducted. If signs of developmental delay were observed, the nurse pointed out in the manual the kinds of activities which were likely to have a salutary effect. Up to the fourth month of life there were no changes in the work protocol; at this time, however, because of the cost involved in weekly visits, the schedule for participants at two outpatient services was changed to every-other-week; in the other services the visits were changed to a monthly schedule. Subsequently, the investigators observed a significant decrease in attendance at all four of the outpatient services. In order to conduct the developmental assessments it was often necessary to make another home visit. By the time the infants were about 10 months of age the protocol was limited to delivery of the monthly manual, evaluation in the outpatient service when possible, and monthly home visits.

Figures 2, 3, and 4 present the main findings concerning the psychomotor development of the infants. The data show that, from about 15 months of age, there was a large and statistically significant difference in the expected direction between the developmental quotients of GE1 and GC1, but there was no difference between GE1 and GC2 (high-income infants). Moreover, up to about 15 months of age, while three out of five comparisons between GE1 and GC1 were

FIGURE 2

Mean Developmental Quotients for GE1, GC1, and GC2

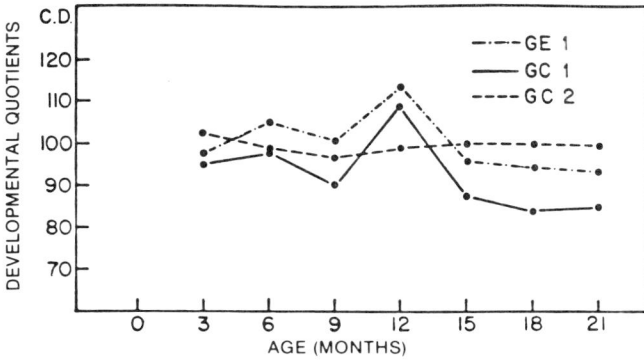

FIGURE 3

Mean Developmental Quotients for GE1, GE3, and GC1

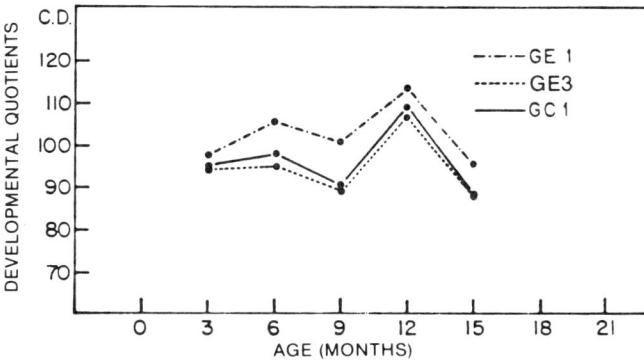

FIGURE 4

Mean Developmental Quotients for GE1, GE2, GE3, and GC1

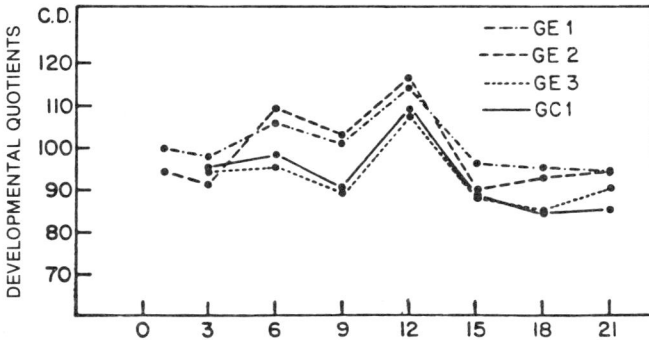

Source: Montenegro et al., 1977.

statistically significant and in the expected direction, the differences were relatively small.

There were no differences between GE1 and GE2; that is, intervention impact was similar whether the program was initiated immediately after birth or at four months of age. More importantly, perhaps, by 21 months there were no differences between GE1 and GE3. Thus, the data do not support the need for intervention during the first months of life; the same results can be obtained by the age of 24 months with interventions that begin at 14 months.

No systematic data were obtained on behavioral changes in caretaking among the mothers during and/or after completion of the study. It is conceivable that the impact of the intervention persisted after termination of the program, so that mothers continued to exhibit the behaviors which had been encouraged. Several nonsystematic observations made following completion of the program indicate that there was behavioral change in the direction of program instructions. Investigators suggest that the behavioral changes among participating women followed a normal curve of distribution; that is, most women showed some change and a few showed either no change or a great many changes in caretaking procedures. Reliable data are a necessity if the effectiveness of this type of intervention strategy is to be assessed.

Plaza Pre-escolar

The report on this program also comes from the staff Mental Health Section of the National Health Service (Montenegro et al., 1977). This four-month project assessed the effectiveness of a "preschool system of education" developed as an alternative to the system currently available in the country. The preschool system introduces changes in both the physical structure to be used and in the educational modality, and it lowers the cost of operation. The investigators were also interested in determining the feasibility of using people and resources from the community in the implementation and conduct of a project dealing with young children.

The methods of procedure for this project were particularly interesting. A plaza (770 sq m) within the community was equipped to meet the needs of the program and served as the project site. Five male and 37 female adolescents (16 to 17 years old) selected from the community were used as monitors in the organization and direction of pedagogical activities for the preschoolers. None had achieved an educational level higher than the second year of secondary school. They each received a small stipend for their work and were supervised by a technical team of nine people. They worked directly

under a formally trained, preschool teacher and a chief monitor.
The program also provided staff to prepare meals and maintain the
center.

The half-day program, two sessions of four hours each, was
divided into a series of directed, semidirected, and free educational
activities. These activities were based on the four center activity
areas: house, art, construction (with blocks, puzzles, etc.), and
workshop. Specific activities in each area included:

house - games involving verbal expression, drama and mime, role-
    playing, story-telling;
art - painting, pasting and construction, shaping of clay, activities
    involving handicrafts (use of hands), games of association and
    classification, building models of real objects;
construction - building with blocks, doing motor exercises and small
    motor development activities, classification activities;
workshop - binding, taking apart, painting, hammering, etc.

The basic philosophy underlying the use of these activities was that
children learn through active manipulation of their environment
(Fundacion de Jardines Infantiles, 1977). The function of the monitors was to lead the children to various activities and materials.

Weekly meetings with parents were organized as part of the
educational program. Parents were divided into groups according
to the age of their children, and meeting content centered around
elementary concepts of child development and behavior, and activities
for stimulating children. Four meetings were held and attending
parents represented approximately 50 percent of the children (Fundacion de Jardines Infantiles, 1977).

The nutritional element of the program consisted of a daily
snack of milk and crackers, fruit, or an egg, and was designed to
cover 25 percent of the children's protein and caloric needs. Health
control and examinations were carried out through the services of
the neighborhood health clinic.

The study design called for pre- and posttreatment evaluation
of an experimental and control group attending a regular kindergarten
class. Each group was divided into two subgroups according to age:
two- to four-year-olds, and four- to five-year-olds (there may have
been some overlap in the subgroups). Development data for the
younger children and intelligence test data for the control group were
analyzed to determine whether variables other than the treatment
affected outcome measures. Intelligence test scores of the untreated
control group, obtained before and after the treatment period of the
experimental group, were compared. The investigators assumed
that if this comparison did not yield statistically significant differences,

and that if the comparison of before and after treatment scores among the index children did yield significant differences, it was an indication that the participation in the Plaza Pre-escolar program had had an effect. As expected, both younger and older index children showed a meaningful gain in both the developmental and intelligence test scores associated with their participation in Plaza Pre-escolar. Posttreatment comparisons between experimental and control children, however, yielded significant differences in the intelligence but not in the developmental scale scores (actual scores are not reported).

Among the qualitative findings a few are worthy of comment. The cost of a "plaza" for this program was estimated by the authors to be about $6,500, reportedly 30 percent of the cost of a regular kindergarten center in Chile. Maintenance costs were estimated to be 54 percent of those in regular kindergartens (Fundacion de Jardines Infantiles, 1977). The use of adolescents from the community as monitors proved to have both advantages and disadvantages in terms of program effects. Their new responsibility led to improved self-motivation for future achievement and possibly to more competent future parenting ability, and they were also enthusiastic teachers. Disadvantages included their limited education and lack of training as teachers. These limitations were reflected in the quality of their interaction with the children and made evident the need for a highly structured monitor training program. Observed changes in the children's behavior included improved self-assurance and increased ability to act on the environment. With respect to the monitors, improvement was noted in their ability to diagnose problems in the children. The strategy described is intriguing and deserves careful analysis, but caution must be exercised in the interpretation and generalization of the data. The project was of short duration and it is unlikely that the developmental changes suggested by the increased IQ scores were deep-rooted. At best, differential test scores represent functional modifications in selective processes of cognition (that is, attention, concentration, memory rehearsal strategies). Theoretically it is improbable that intervention of such short duration could result in modifications in the learning capabilities of children. Regarding community participation in the project, it would be helpful to determine whether or not active interest could be maintained over an extended period of time; four years, perhaps, rather than four months.

Project Parents and Children

This is a parent education project whose purpose is to foster the intellectual competence and physical growth of young children in rural Chile. Specific objectives are to assist parents to develop: caretaking skills for stimulating the young child; attitudes conducive to creating a healthy atmosphere for child-rearing; and motivation to act on their environment on behalf of their children (CIDE, 1976; Whelan et al., 1977).

The project is being run by staff from the Center for Research and Development in Education (Centro de Investigacion y Desarrollo de la Educacion, CIDE), a semipublic research agency that receives support from the public sector. Both a pilot and an experimental project are located in a rural area of central Chile, in the valley of Aconcagua. It is an area characterized by high primary school drop-out rates, limited parental education (59 percent of parents in the program had less than a complete primary education), economic activity dependent on small farming, and a notably young population age structure. Total duration of the project is two years.

The rural primary schools in the area were used as bases of operation and selected primary teachers served as parent educators. Scheduled meetings with parents were devoted to work on specific themes: environmental factors influencing the development of the child; visual-motor development; development of biological functions; development of language; effective parent-child interaction; nutrition; sexual education; and the effects on the child of alcohol ingestion by the mother during pregnancy. These themes emerged from a questionnaire, administered during the pilot phase of the program, that investigated areas of parental interest and concern.

Ten schools in the department of San Felipe (five experimental and five control) were selected for involvement in the program. The investigators were particularly interested in working with a representative rural sample; therefore, they eliminated special schools and schools in urban zones or in areas with unusually large populations. Two teachers from each school participated in the experimental part of the program, as did 60 mothers with children from four to six years of age. Selection of both teachers and mothers was made from volunteer families in participating schools.

The training program for parent educators was conducted in 25 sessions requiring a total of 40 hours. Specific themes were discussed at each meeting; for example, overall project philosophy, methodology, factors operating in a rural environment that could be expected to act as obstacles to normal child development. The training program was supervised by a technical team of 12 persons who worked part-time designing and testing materials, training, and supervising the sessions.

Teachers met with participating mothers once a week, for 59 sessions, to develop a series of themes. The approach appeared to follow the adult literacy techniques developed by Paulo Freire (1970,

1973). During each session the subject theme was broken down into working units of ideas or information. A theme, or unit, was introduced by a series of slides or pictures depicting problematical situations, and these served as bases for discussions of concrete problems or issues, directly or indirectly related to the situation of the young child. Each slide series was accompanied by a teacher's guide that presented objectives and possible lines of discussion. The objective of the sessions was to help the mothers develop new ideas and skills in caretaking practices, and to become aware of themselves as deliberate teachers of their children. Part of each session was also devoted to demonstrations of how mothers could construct materials for stimulating their children.

As part of the evaluation protocol, children of participating mothers were tested before, midway into, and at the end of the project. Two groups of rural children, matched with the experimental group for education of parents, were used as controls and one of these groups was exposed to kindergarten programs. The test used in the evaluation was the Wechsler Intelligence Scale for Preschool Children (Filp et al., 1977) which had been standardized on an urban Chilean population. In November 1977 the authors reported results of preliminary testing on the experimental and kindergarten groups at 0, 4, and 8 months of treatment. It was hypothesized that after 8 months both the experimental and kindergarten groups would show significant increases on their Wechsler IQ, and that there would be no significant differences between these groups. An analysis was conducted using the total Wechsler scores at 0, 4, and 8 months as a base. Of the principal effects analyzed, only time proved to be statistically significant. After eight months of treatment the experimental group showed an increase of 7.6 points and the control group an increase of 6 points on the Wechsler. There were no significant between-group differences (Filp et al., 1977). The authors interpreted these tentative findings as suggesting that the experimental treatment with the mothers had a significant effect on the intellectual development of their children; one comparable to the effects of a formal kindergarten program.

Only 18 experimental and 17 control children were tested and one of the control groups had only six children; therefore, the findings must be qualified due to inadequate sample size. In addition, given possible measurement errors, the small increase (7.6 and 6 points, respectively) is of questionable significance.

Changes in attitudes and behaviors of the mothers were to be measured by a structural questionnaire administered before, during, and after the program. No data are available on the effects of the program on participating mothers except the impressions of the investigators that the nutrition theme had the greatest effect on their home behavior, as well as being the theme they enjoyed most (CIDE, 1976).

COLOMBIA

Intelligent Children Program

This research-service community program was directed at low-income parents and represents an effort to work with them, under relatively structured conditions, on selected topics in the areas of nutrition, health, and psychosocial stimulation of their 0- to 24-month-old infants. The broadening of parental caretaking skills relative to the developmental needs of children was basic to the program, as was the need to protect their well-being and facilitate their physical growth. The program operated in Rincon de Suba, a low-income barrio Bogota, Colombia (CEDEN/FEPEC, 1976, 1977a) and was implemented by the Center for the Development of Nonformal Education, one of the units of the Foundation for Lifelong Learning. Program planning was initiated in December 1975 and was concluded in April 1978.

The research component focused primarily on evaluating the effectiveness of the intervention strategy. The development of a model for nonformal education of parents was a more ambitious projected achievement. From a service perspective the goal was to implement or strengthen caretaking skills among parents, which would then be used to optimize the growth and development of their children. The program operated on the basis of what was described as an educational model and its subject matter, didactic material, and methods had well-defined, discrete objectives (Toro et al., 1977).

Two manuals were developed, one for health and the other for psychosocial stimulation. Topics in the former included identification of malnutrition, the relationship between malnutrition and mental development, interactions between nutrition and infection, breast-feeding, vaccinations, and use of health services. The psychosocial manual included approximately 300 activities and games that families could use with their infants. These activities were divided into six chapters based on the chronological age of the children.

The materials used to transmit the educational messages to parents were considered to be of primary importance by those responsible for the project. Some of them were created and prepared by the staff, some were adapted from other projects. Among the printed materials, one of the most ingenious and useful was The Baby Book. Parents used it to record chronologically the developmental landmarks attained by their children and events which were of particular significance to them. The book could be used to describe the rate of development of an infant and may also have had a positive reinforcement effect on the parents. Photographic slides were also used to communicate selected caretaking messages to parents. Two sets of slides were prepared, one centered on the area of nutrition and health and the other on infant stimulation.

An initial phase of the project was restricted to group actions which centered on the discussion of selected topics concerning growth and development. Participating families were originally divided into three groups according to the ages of the infants: G1—0 to 4 months old; G2—4 to 8 months old; and G3—8 to 12 months old. In a second phase all groups were clustered together and met weekly in a church within the community. These new meetings also centered around specific developmental issues and audio-visual aids were used to transmit the educational messages.

Evaluation data from the project are still quite limited, but a preliminary midpoint evaluation of the progress of participating mothers has been conducted (CEDEN/FEPEC, 1977a). A criterion referenced questionnaire, based on the content of the curriculum guides, was developed and administered to 105 mothers. The purpose was to measure changes in the mothers' knowledge and behavior in the areas of nutrition, health, and infant stimulation. Although it is not clear how the questionnaire was able to measure behavior, the findings indicated that mothers scored 67 percent of a "maximum" possible score on nutrition and health knowledge, 62 percent on nutrition and health behavior, 37 percent on stimulation knowledge, and 58 percent on stimulation behavior. In spite of the relatively lower scores on the stimulation component, the CEDEN evaluation team argues that the "net" gain was greater because the area of infant stimulation was the one in which mothers had the least knowledge and expertise when the project began. They also suggest that progress in the areas of nutrition and health was impeded by socioeconomic factors outside the mothers' control (CEDEN/FEPEC, 1977a).

As part of their examination, the CEDEN team compared the scores of mothers who had attended various numbers of sessions. They established five groups: No. 1 attended no sessions (n = 5), No. 2 attended 1-5 sessions (n = 32), No. 3 attended 6-10 sessions (n = 27), No. 4 attended 11-20 sessions (n = 32), and No. 5 attended 21-30 sessions (n = 9). Significant differences in the expected direction in nutrition and health behavior were found only between group 1 (no attendance) and group 5 (attendance at 21-30 sessions); no significant differences were found between group 5 and groups 2, 3, or 4. In general, the largest differences due to attendance were found in the area of infant stimulation knowledge and behavior. Significant differences in nutrition and health knowledge were also found between groups 1 and 5. On the average, the majority of mothers attended only half of the 30 sessions.

Some impressionistic findings were that, through involvement in the program, mothers were learning to identify potential developmental

problems and were also interacting more among themselves with respect to ideas and practices for encouraging attendance at the sessions
(CEDEN, 1976). Problems were noted in several areas: cooperation
between CEDEN and ICBF on various aspects of the project, teacher
reliability, and attendance.

An additional objective of the project was to determine whether
any effect on children's developmental scale scores resulted from
educating the parents. For this purpose the investigators established
baseline scores through pretreatment evaluation (CEDEN/FEPEC,
1977a). These data show that, although the developmental quotients
in the Griffith Scale of the children are slightly below the standard,
the scores are well within normal range. Indeed, it seems unlikely
that the standard and sample means would differ at a statistically
significant level. The means for the sample run from 95.43 (s.d. =
17.78) in the auditory-language area to 99.47 (s.d. = 17.08) in the
locomotor area. Given this baseline, and if the development of these
children does not tend to be retarded, it might be difficult for the
investigators to detect subsequent treatment effects on these developmental scores.

Home Care Centers

This pilot program was developed in La Candelaria, a low-
income community in Cartegena, Colombia. Under the guidance of
paraprofessional teachers, it attempted to examine the efficacy of
providing low-cost custodial care and simple educational activities,
as well as lunch and a snack, to barriada children two to four years
of age (Berrueta-Clements, Flores, and Aurora, 1977).

The project design did not include an evaluation component.
The program operated under the auspices of the Oficina de Rehabilitacion de Tugurios in Cartegena, a government community development agency, and external support was provided by UNICEF. Program services were directed chiefly towards children of working
mothers in La Candelaria. Area families were generally large,
averaging four or five children; there was a high unemployment rate,
and a high proportion of fatherless families. Most women worked
outside the home as ambulatory vendors, market women, domestics,
laundry women, and so on. The houses were usually constructed of
mud and bricks and, while many had electricity, most lacked water
and hygienic facilities. Young children were unclothed or minimally
dressed and generally without shoes.

In early 1977 each of the three home care centers operating
in La Candelaria provided care for approximately ten children. The
centers were also used at various times by infants as young as six

months and neighborhood children from eight to ten years of age.
The teacher-caretaker of each home center was a young woman from
the community who had been trained in basic child care and stimulation techniques. Paraprofessional teachers and mothers, as well as
the mother whose home was being used, learned teaching skills by
observing the two Catholic nuns who worked with the children. In
addition, several nuns, involved with the program in supervisory
capacities, worked with the paraprofessional teachers.

In March 1977 Juan Berrueta-Clements, Aurora, and Flores
informally evaluated the program by observation and interview.
They reported that the caretakers seemed to provide adequate care
with respect to meeting the children's physical needs and that the
young participants worked well with each other and with the adults.
The latter suggests that the home care situation provided an opportunity for socialization into group work skills.

Educational stimulation within the program was not clearly
defined and consisted mainly of large group activities initiated by an
adult. These activities accounted for only two of the eight hours of
child care. There appeared to be no set curriculum for the project
and activities were chosen in a haphazard manner. It was reported
that older neighborhood children sometimes participated actively
with center participants and were successful in setting up games and
activities for all. Otherwise the tendency was for the teacher and/or
supervising nun to be active and the children passive in various
learning activities. The project showed no incidence of purposeful
daily or weekly planning of educational activities.

The homes being used in the project were reportedly clean,
had ample space for the children, and, in spite of problems in much
of the barrio, had adequate sanitary facilities. While there appeared
to be a limited but adequate amount of educational materials in the
homes, the children did not have sufficient access to them.

One of the program objectives was to determine the most cost
effective way of providing both child care and stimulation while rely-
ing on community resources, both human and financial, as much as
possible. Until now the program has been running with external support from UNICEF and, therefore, it is difficult to draw conclusions
about the effectiveness of its strategy with regard to being self-sustaining. Officials from the Oficina de Rehabilitacion de Tugurios
report a monthly operating cost of 500 pesos per child, an amount
far in excess of what most families could afford to pay for child care
services. Average family income in the barriada in which the program is located is 1,000 pesos per month.

Currently, 80 percent of program costs goes to buying food
for lunch and snacks. It is reported that the nutritional supplementation received by the children is of good quality, but no details are

available on specific foods used or nutritional requirements met (Berrueta-Clements, Flores, and Aurora, 1977). The question of decreasing the cost of this element of the program, without decreasing its quality, is crucial if the program is to be self-sustaining.

PERU

Experimental Stimulation Program

This program was developed in order to examine the effectiveness of specially designed intervention activities on the cognitive development of children of low socioeconomic background (Majluf, 1972). The largest population was from barriadas in Lima and was already attending regular programs of initial education. The program attempted to examine the cognitive benefits of having teachers provide increased attention to individual needs, and was thus a research effort within Peru's national public early intervention program (see Chapter 8). The basis of treatment was a curriculum normally used in special education programs for mildly retarded children.

The program was carried out in five initial Education centers in the shanty towns and marginal urban zones of Lima. Experimental and control groups were selected from among children in the centers who had demonstrated, on previously administered tests (Majluf, 1971), clear evidence of intellectual immaturity and low IQ. These same tests were used as pre- and posttests in the program. They included the ABC test of reading and writing readiness developed by Lawrence Filho, which consists of eight subtests measuring maturity on skills which form the basis of reading and writing ability; the Jordan-Massey test of mental abilities; and the Harris-Goodenough draw-a-figure test. Originally there were 25 experimental and 25 control children, but by the end of the program only 21 experimental and 14 controls remained. No explanation is provided for the 15 children who dropped out of the program.

The treatment lasted from May to November and consisted of one hour daily of special activities conducted by the regular teacher, but in a separate classroom. The teachers were each assigned approximately four children and worked with each on those activities and skills on which the child had tested lowest. The curriculum included language, visuo-motor, auditory, tactile, sensory, and classificatory activities broken down into four levels of graduated difficulty. The program also used materials on reading and writing readiness, mathematical skills, and a set of materials identified as "Developmental Learning Materials" (Majluf, 1972, pp. 5-7). The control children continued with their normal program.

Both groups demonstrated evidence of growth in skills and abilities between May and the posttest in December. The experimental group, which in May had exhibited lower scores than the control group on all three tests, demonstrated significantly greater growth in terms of intragroup differences in test scores. On the Jordan-Massey test the experimental group had a 24-point gain from May to December, and the control group a 16-point gain (51 to 75 versus 59 to 75). The magnitude of difference in gain between the two groups was significant at the .025 level. On the ABC test the experimental group demonstrated a four-point gain (8.5 to 12.5), the control group a 2.8-point gain. Here magnitude of the difference was not significant. On the Harris-Goodenough test the gain was 13.5 points for the experimental group, and 5.6 for the control group (80.7 to 94.2 versus 81 to 86.6). The magnitude of difference in gain between the two groups was significant at the .025 level.

An important question left unanswered by the evaluation is whether or not the extra progress made by the children in the experimental group was worth the enormous time and effort involved. Five well-trained teachers were needed to foster moderate gains in 21 children, while control children, through participation in the regular Initial Education program, demonstrated almost as much progress in the same time period. In other words, moderately greater gains on selected tests were made only at the cost of disproportionately greater investment of human and financial resources.

The experimental program was repeated from May to November 1974 in expanded form and using a slightly different methodology (Majluf, 1974). The experimental group was expanded to 80 and the control to 50. Treatment was similar to that used in 1972 but was divided into three content areas: global and segmentary psychomotor skills, sensory-perceptual skills, and communication skills. All activities were graduated in difficulty. The program reportedly followed the theoretical lines of the cognitive-oriented curriculum developed by D. Weihart at the High/Scope Foundation in Ypsilanti, Michigan.

Briefly, the results again indicated that the children in the experimental group made greater gains than did children in the control group, although the latter started off with slightly higher scores. The magnitude of the difference in gain between experimental and low-income control groups was significant for all but the ABC test.

CONCLUSION

This chapter highlights the diversity of the intervention strategies which have been explored in programs for low-income preschool children. Few of these projects share common modes of operation, yet all report beneficial effects on recipients. It is impressive to note that despite differences in budgets, and most likely in methodological adequacy, these community projects and the quasi-experimental studies (Chapter 4) report similar positive efforts. Perhaps the only exception is in the case of infants 12 months of age or younger, for whom benefits have not been clearly shown. Indeed, it was noted in the Plaza Pre-escolar study that the effects of interventions beginning at birth and at 14 months are similar.

An intriguing inference that emerges from the findings reviewed is that the methods used to improve cognitive development of young children are not critical; that is, children appear to benefit from either direct or indirect approaches. In terms of gains in intelligence scale scores, it is equally beneficial to work with the child in a day care center or with the mother at home. The implications of these findings are enormous, not only because working with mothers may be less costly, but also because it allows them to develop skills which are useful in coping with a variety of family problems.

The data reviewed produce a certain amount of optimism. They demonstrate the extraordinary plasticity of the human organism and show how its developmental course can be shaped in part by environmental engineering. At the same time it is distressing to find that the focus of these studies is restricted to intrafamily conditions. With the possible exception of the CIDE project, the studies do not attempt to relate the conditions of the family to the social and economic inequities of the society that creates them.

The findings reported must be interpreted with great caution. In behavioral science, changes in IQ or other behavioral measurements over months do not necessarily demonstrate long-lasting changes. Indeed, behavioral measures often suggest that treatment effects disappear with retesting simply because of statistical artifacts. In connection with the projects reviewed, there are no data to show that the changes associated with treatment will last. In the case of the Plaza Pre-escolar program, for example, the effects reported following short-term treatments (4 months) are suspect and may well have disappeared if the children had been retested later.

Finally, some of these projects point out that their interventions need not be viewed exclusively as exercises in child development. Several of them report successful communication and collaboration with the community; in some cases members of the community worked in the implementation of the pedagogical activities. Thus, by the very nature of their activities these projects become strategies for community development.

6
CASE STUDY 1:
ANTIOQUIA, COLOMBIA

It is clear from material presented earlier that the mental development of a child born and raised in an economically impoverished environment, where malnutrition is endemic, is in double jeopardy. First, because the child has little chance to take advantage of the formal education system, the opportunity to develop the skills required by an industrial society is limited. Second, because of constant exposure to the adverse biological and social conditions associated with poverty, it is unlikely that the child's intellect will be developed to its fullest potential. Previous chapters have established that, in comparison to middle- or high-income children, the low-income child is less likely to perform well on tests of intelligence or cognitive skills.

Despite a few contradictory findings, evidence also indicates that the cognitive deficits of the low-income child may be prevented or ameliorated by comprehensive intervention programs. Although many questions remain regarding optimal intervention strategy, and additional information is required before final conclusions can be drawn, it has been shown that interventions linking nutrition, health, and education are beneficial to the development of the child even after the third year of life.

Given these conditions, it is conceivable that intervention programs of these types may become priority tasks for interested governments. Such programs may be viewed as methods for attending to the basic needs of the population and, as such, may represent a strategy for social and economic development (Selowsky, 1976). These programs are also likely to be extremely attractive to impoverished families who are cognizant of the developmental handicaps of which their children are at risk.

The case of Colombia is illustrative in this regard. In 1974, under the assumption that poverty and malnutrition have an adverse

70

effect on the mental development of young children, the Parliament approved Law 27. This mandate called for the creation of Centers for Integrated Attention for Preschool Children (CAIP) for infants and preschool children of public and private employees, the self-employed, and the unemployed. While these centers are cited as evidence of the commitment of the government to social and economic equity, the development of the program poses serious financial problems. The number of legitimate candidates for these services is large: for example, in the municipality of Medellin alone the number exceeds 130,000 children. The cost of such an enterprise for the entire country lies in the millions of dollars.

The most effective way to assess the need for infant and preschool programs in Latin America may be to describe the nature and magnitude of poverty, in representative countries, in a way which focuses attention on the situation of the young child. Chapter 1, an initial step in this process, dealt with statistical estimates of absolute and relative poverty and with related demographic projections. This and the two following chapters continue the process by discussing, in greater depth, the conditions of young children in Colombia, Peru, and Venezuela. Moreover, in each of these chapters the respective descriptive data on the conditions of poverty are antecedents to the descriptions of large-scale intervention programs in these three countries. The criteria for the selection of Colombia, Peru, and Venezuela for case study sites were: (1) geographic and cultural diversity; (2) existence of preschool intervention programs of relatively large coverage; and (3) availability of personnel to conduct the field studies in each of these three locations.

In preparation for the field studies, the investigator reviewed literature on various aspects of life in the selected regions. Particular emphasis was given to a number of documents, generally unpublished, on the problems of young children. This review could be carried out only after visits to the sites because many of the relevant documents were unavailable in the United States. Next, on-site observations lasting from three to six weeks were carried out. Interviews were held with officials in both the public and private sectors. In the case of Venezuela, a questionnaire covering certain aspects of the programs visited was completed during each of the interviews and descriptive notes were taken. The third and final stage involved data analysis and preparation of the case studies.

DEMOGRAPHIC CHARACTERISTICS

Colombia's population is the third largest in South America, and is growing at a rate of 3 percent annually (USAID/Colombia, 1974);

the projected population for the year 2000 is 42 million (CELADE, 1978). At that time children from 0 to 15 years of age will represent 35.1 percent of the population, or 14.1 million persons. In 1975 the population under 6 years of age made up 17.7 percent of the total population, or 4.2 million; by the year 2000 this age group will represent 14.5 percent of the population and will number approximately 6.2 million (Galofre, 1979).

The majority of Colombia's 23 million people (1976 estimate, Sewell, 1977) inhabit the Caribbean seaboard and the two highland valley areas of the Andean Cordillera. The eastern part of the country, 50 percent of Colombia's land area, is largely unpopulated; it contains only 1.5 percent of the population in its nine territories. Colombia is undergoing rapid urbanization, with four major cities (Bogota, Medellin, Cali, and Barranquilla) absorbing half the country's annual population growth. The 5-6 percent annual urban growth rate is more than twice the rural rate (Vallejo Mejia, 1975). Current estimates put the urban population of Colombia at 67 percent of the total population (IDB, 1975).

The migration to the temperate, highland urban areas places enormous social pressure on these centers. Bogota is probably the most severely strained, and it has not responded in terms of industrial expansion, provision of services, or planning for the migration trend (Parra Sandoval, 1973). Even taking these deficits into account, urban socioeconomic development has surpassed that of rural zones.

SOCIOECONOMIC CONDITIONS

Even though the GNP growth rate per capita is 3.4 percent annually, slightly higher than the population growth rate, and per capita GNP is close to $500, the inequity of income distribution is striking. One estimate indicates that the top 5 percent of wage earners receive 35 percent of the national income, while the bottom 50 percent receive 14 percent (Aguirrezabal, DeTrujillo, and Botero, 1976) (see also Table 2, Chapter 1). Another report states that the highest paid 10 percent and the lowest paid 6 percent of the population receive 44 and 25 percent, respectively, of the income (Berry and Urrutia, 1976). In the rural areas the top 10 percent actually receives 55 percent of the income. A recent estimate places average rural sector wages at $23 monthly, and urban sector wages at $54 monthly (Berry and Urrutia, 1976). A majority of the estimated 650,000 known unemployed and 800,000 underemployed are rural migrants in search of work in the industrial sector (Aguirrezabal, DeTrujillo, and Botero, 1976; Vallejo Mejia, 1975).

Since approximately 75 percent of Colombia's population is living in moderate to severe poverty (Vallejo Mejia, 1975), and since the pregnancy rate of low-income women 15 to 24 years of age is estimated to be about five times that of middle- and upper-income women (Agualimpia, 1969), it can be estimated that more than half of the young children in Colombia live in conditions of moderate to severe poverty. In 1975, for example, the Colombian Institute of Family Welfare (ICBF) in Antioquia determined that, of the 1,162,444 people making up the population of the municipality of Medellin, 260,923 (22.45 percent) were children between zero and seven years of age. More than half of this number (132,389) came from households that had no fixed income or whose annual income was less than 2,200 Colombian pesos ($65).

NUTRITION AND HEALTH

Although estimates suggest that the average daily per capita availability of colories is relatively adequate (2,251), one-fifth of the population consumes 60 percent or less of the recommended minimum requirements, and protein availability is 17 percent under the 41.7 gram recommended allowance (World Bank, 1977). As might be expected, there is a positive covariation between the adequacy of calories, proteins, vitamin, and mineral intake, and socioeconomic level (Paez-Franco, 1973).

As in other areas of social concern, nutritional conditions in rural areas are worse than in urban areas. A 1977 World Bank report indicates that in the 1960s the daily per capita calorie intake for the rural poor was 1,538 grams and the protein intake was 30 grams. For middle-class urban dwellers during the same period the figures were 3,138 calories and 54 grams of protein (Paez-Franco, 1973).

Protein-calorie malnutrition affects about four million children, or two-thirds of those under 7 years of age, and approximately 22 percent of children under 4 suffer moderate to severe malnutrition (World Bank, 1977). The nutrition division of the ICBF estimates that malnutrition effects 746,000 urban and 367,000 rural children, or 60.5 percent of the population under 2 years of age (USAID/Colombia, 1976). Puffer and Serrano (1973) report that nurtitional deficiency is an underlying or associated cause of death in children under 5 in 36.4, 44.7, and 42.3 percent of cases examined in three Colombian cities. Other nutritional problems prevalent among young children include avitaminosis (particularly lack of Vitamin A), calcium deficiency, and iron deficiency anemia (Paez-Franco, 1973; World Bank, 1977).

A World Bank study (1977) cited the mortality rate for infants and young children as 70 per 1,000 live births; and the International Development Bank (1975) had estimated it to be 93.8 per 1,000 live births. Deaths of children zero to four years of age make up 40 percent of all deaths and those of children under one year of age, 28 percent of all deaths (World Bank, 1977). A USAID report (USAID/Colombia, 1974) indicates that of 18 Latin American countries Colombia has the highest death rate from infectious and parasitic diseases among the one to four year age group.

EDUCATION

The limited educational opportunities which have been available for young children traditionally have been offered in departmental capitals and other urban settings. Although the situation is changing in response to the increased interest of governmental and private groups in the needs of this segment of the population, only a few experimental efforts reflect changes in strategy, philosophy, or target population.

The first public kindergartens were built in selected cities in 1962 and served only a few hundred students, mainly children of working mothers from poor neighborhoods. By 1971 there were 28 public kindergartens and approximately 1,415 private kindergartens, the latter serving 95,000 children. One-third of the private centers were in Bogota and all served a basically upper-class population. By 1974 there were 172 public kindergartens serving 6,000 children, presumably those from low-income families (Bernard Van Leer Foundation, 1976a).

In 1971 only 26 of every 1,000 middle school students were from rural areas; of every 1,000 university students, one was from a rural area (Hoxeng, 1973). In urban areas 507 of every 1,000 children who enter primary school reach fifth grade; in rural areas the figure falls to 40 (Perez Sanin, 1976). A 1975 Ministry of Education report (Parra Sandoval, 1973) shows that in rural zones 76 percent of primary schools have only one classroom; 80 percent have only one teacher; only 32 percent of rural teachers have graduated from college; and 80 percent of rural primary schools are limited to two or three grades. Forty percent of rural Colombian children never attend school at all. The literacy rate in Colombia is estimated to be 77.6 percent (IDB, 1975). When the functionally illiterate, those whose education is limited to one or two years of primary school, are removed from this group, however, the rate drops to approximately 50 percent.

The above description indicates that preschool education is essentially nonexistent for the estimated three million children in "dire" need of such services (Bernard Van Leer Foundation, 1976a). At a maximum, there may be 10,000 children enrolled in public preschool programs in Colombia, although, as indicated, thousands of middle- and upper-class children attend private programs. It is also important to note that services currently offered are almost exclusively the province of those in urban settings.

YOUNG CHILD POLICY IN COLOMBIA

Colombia has a long history of concern for the welfare of its children. In 1946 the Parliament enacted Law 83, an important precursor of Law 27, which is studied in this chapter. This initial legislative document asserted the legal rights of children and detailed the welfare assistance they were to receive in cases of abandonment and deprivation. Article 69 of the law specified that it was the right of any child in Colombia to benefit from those conditions necessary for healthy physical growth and moral, social, and intellectual development (Jurisdiccion de Menores, 1976).

Following the enactment of Law 83, a National Council for the Protection of Children was formed. The council operated through departments or local communities in various regions of the country. Its objective was to provide assistance to pregnant women, mothers, infants, and young children. The law also specified that all public organizations and other institutions which received government support should provide the council with the assistance necessary to fulfill its objectives. In essence the council became the coordinator of all activities developed on behalf of preschool children.

In December 1968 a new legal disposition (ICBF/Law 75) was enacted by the Parliament on behalf of children and their families. It mandated the formation of the Colombian Institute of Family Welfare (ICBF), which was to function as an autonomous public institution. The ICBF then absorbed the National Council for the Protection of Children and incorporated activities of the latter into its program. In 1969 the National Institute of Nutrition, which had been formed in 1963, was integrated into ICBF (Paez-Franco, 1973). The 1968 law also specified that the Ministries of Agriculture, Health, and National Education should coordinate their activities with ICBF in order to: (1) provide adequate prenatal care; (2) improve the quality of the dietary intake of mothers during lactation; (3) disseminate school feeding programs; (4) provide services for preventive medicine within the school system; and (5) extend hospital and nutritional rehabilitation services to children.

Law 27, approved by the Parliament in 1974, mandated creation of Centers for Integrated Attention for Preschool Children (CAIPs)
to serve the children of public or private employees, the self-employed,
and the unemployed. Funds allocated for the creation and organization of these centers were to be equivalent to 2 percent of the payrolls
of all public and private institutions.

Following enactment of the law in December 1974, the regional
offices of the Colombian Institute of Family Welfare (ICBF) became
responsible for the creation of the CAIPs. The office located in the
department of Antioquia appeared to be the most successful in carrying out the mandate. Of approximately 410 centers operating throughout the country in 1977, 105 of them were within this department. It
was decided, therefore, to assess the implementation of the law by
focusing on an area noted for its success in carrying out the CAIP
program.

THE ANTIOQUIA SETTING

The data obtained on the economic characteristics of the population selected for the field study are more detailed for Medellin than
for the overall department. Accordingly, after a brief overall description, the following discussion focuses on the municipality of
Medellin and the six communes, or administrative zones, which
form it.

The department of Antioquia is located in the northwest region
of Colombia and its 62,870 square kilometers represent 5.5 percent
of the total land area of the country. It borders the sea of Antillas,
and the departments of Bolivar, Sucre, and Cordoba in the north;
Caldas and Risaralda in the south; Santander and Boyaca in the east;
and Chaco in the west.

Antioquia is subdivided into ten administrative subregions and
109 municipalities, 75 percent of which can be considered rural,
given the definition of a rural area as a locus of less than 2,500 persons (Marshall and Paul, 1970). In 1973 the population of the department was 2,950,550 and the population density was 47 inhabitants per
square kilometer. Only the department of Cundinamarca (population
3,961,691), in which Bogota is located, is more heavily populated.
Medellin, the capital of Antioquia, is the center of all government
activities and bears the greatest administrative responsibility. In
1976 there were an estimated 1,320,921 persons in Medellin, and
the population growth rate was 4.39 percent, one of the highest among
Latin American cities (Gobernacion de Antioquia, 1976).

The department of Antioquia in general and the municipality
of Medellin in particular are two of the most important industrial

centers in Colombia. Their economic growth has been rapid and, with the exception of Cundinamarca, employment rates compare favorably with all other regions. Despite this comparably satisfactory situation, an analysis of the statistical data for Medellin, by the Departamento Administrativo de Planeacion y Servicios Tecnicos (1977), indicates that a large segment of the population lives in extreme poverty. For example, in commune number 1, which includes a total of 35 neighborhoods and 283,589 inhabitants, the highest average household incomes range from 3,000 to 4,000 Colombian pesos ($88-$117) per month. At least nine of these neighborhoods, with a total of approximately 50,000 people, have an average household income of 1,500 pesos ($44) per month. Households average six to seven persons; therefore, the per capita monthly income among these latter families is approximately 250 pesos ($7). Of the 177,069 households in the municipality of Medellin, 42,047 have no fixed income, 39,665 have monthly incomes of less than 2,200 Colombian pesos ($64) (ICBF/Antioquia, 1975), and it is estimated that nearly 70 percent of the households have incomes insufficient to provide the basic necessities of food, health, and housing.

If attention is focused on children, the situation is even more bleak. Children six years of age or younger total 260,923 and represent 22.4 percent of the population of the municipality. More than 110,000 live in households with no fixed incomes or with monthly incomes of less than 2,200 pesos ($64). In addition, 22,324 children live in squatter settlements or in the rural section of the municipality (ICBF/Antioquia, 1975).

By 1977 the literacy rate for the department of Antioquia was approximately 80 percent. This figure compares favorably with the rate for the rest of the country, which was 77.6 percent when measured in 1974 (IDB, 1975). The school-age population (5 to 19 years of age) amounts to 861,075, although total enrollment in both public and private schools, from preschool through secondary years, accounts for only 392,316, or less than 50 percent of the eligible population. School wastage is a significant part of the problem. In Medellin in 1976 10 percent of enrollees dropped out during the academic year. The drop-out rate reaches 74 percent in rural areas (Departamento Administrativo de Planeacion y Servicios Tecnicos, 1977).

LAW 27 AND THE CAIPs

The responsibility for carrying out the mandate of the law falls on ICBF; therefore, this report focuses on a descriptive analysis of the philosophy, administration, and modes of operation of the CAIPs in Medellin and Antioquia.

A primary concept of Law 27 is that of integrated attention in the formation of the CAIPs. Two different, but possibly complementary, meanings of integrated attention are apparent from an analysis of the documentation for the program. The first is inferred from the text and description of the law, and from the operation of the CAIPs themselves. It refers to the nature and coordination of the services provided to the child and family: health, nutrition, and education. In this context, integrated attention refers to a concern for, and support of, the biological, physical, and sociopsychological health and development of the child; that is, a holistic view of the development of the organism. To illustrate, in this context, malnutrition refers not only to a biophysical problem, but also to a problem in the child's psychological development.

The second meaning of integrated attention emerges from an internal ICBF document: Philosophy of Integrated Attention (ICBF, 1977). This paper focuses on the sociopsychological conditions that must exist in the CAIPs in order to foster "normal" growth and development of the children. As spelled out in this document, normality does not refer to any arbitrary set of statistical criteria, but to exogenous and endogenous conditions that exist whenever development occurs naturally. This sociopsychological perspective calls for a departure from traditional preschool education strategies that have prepared children for primary schooling by developing reading and writing skills, and promoting the submissive attitudes valued by teachers and other significant adults. In contrast, the notion of integrated attention focuses on the development of an autonomous personality, and logical, motor, and linguistic abilities. These are to be fulfilled by creating an environment in the CAIPs which effectively substitutes for that of the family. Accordingly, the caretaker or nursery school teacher is a mother surrogate who optimizes environmental conditions for constant and fruitful interaction among children and adults.

The integrated approach described above focuses on interrelationships in the social, emotional, and cognitive worlds of the child and seeks integration among them. In this context the environment is viewed as a moderator of such integration, and emphasis is placed on shaping that environment. This working strategy is based on a concept of developmental plasticity and susceptibility to outside influence.

Administrative Infrastructure

Within ICBF the responsibility for the organization and coordination of the CAIPs throughout the country has been assigned to the Office of Social Promotion; the subdirector of this office in ICBF in Bogota is the chief coordinator for the entire CAIP operation. A Central Council of Administration is the ultimate authority for the program and sets policy throughout the country. The council includes the president of ICBF, the minister of labor and social security or his representative, the minister of health or his representative, and representatives of the employers' and the employees' associations. The director of ICBF may assist and speak in the council, but has no vote.

Regional offices are responsible for the actual implementation of the program. In Antioquia, the director of the Office of Social Promotion within ICBF in Medellin is the chief coordinator. He is directly responsible to both the regional director of ICBF and the subdirector of the Office of Social Promotion in Bogota. A professional staff of psychologists, sociologists, dieticians, educators, and nurses provide technical support to the coordinator and serve as a liaison between both the central and zonal offices, as well as the administrative entities operating individual CAIPs. The Regional Council of Administration has similar functions and organization and serves as a liaison between regional organizations and the Central Council in Bogota.

The ICBF office in Antioquia capitalized on the preschool centers (for example, nursery schools or other infant centers for custodial care) in carrying out the mandate of Law 27, thus taking advantage of facilities and personnel already available. The ICBF office provided financial and technical support to these preexisting centers so they could meet the administrative and technical requirements defined by the central ICBF office in Bogota. In most cases, ICBF made contractual arrangements with organizations experienced in the administration of preschool programs. For example, ICBF developed a working arrangement with ACAIPA, a private nonprofit organization which directed the activities of 34 preschool centers. To ensure that each child received integrated attention, ICBF provided funding and, where necessary, technical assistance, while ACAIPA relied on their own administrative infrastructure to operate the program.

In addition, ICBF developed new CAIPs, without support from any preexisting organizations. In some instances, parents initiated the organization and then requested financial and technical support to aid them in developing a CAIP. In these cases, administrative responsibility lay with the parents, but staff make-up and mode of operation were determined by ICBF requirements.

As of October 30, 1977, the Central Office of Antioquia had allocated 380,421,826 Colombian pesos ($11,026,719) for the development of 112 CAIPs, 85 of which were in operation and providing services to approximately 7,000 children. In addition, 73,610,940 pesos ($2,133,650) had been allocated to 62 institutions that had been functioning as preschool centers and which, after the enactment of the law, began to operate within the CAIP philosophy. These centers provided assistance to 4,000 children.

Within the CAIPs three levels of personnel carry out activities with attending children. The director is responsible primarily for the administrative and technical aspects of the program as specified by ICBF. He is also responsible for preparation and administration of the budget and for serving as a liaison between the center and the regional office. The technical staff works directly with the children in the center and is required to follow ICBF specifications for the provision of integrated attention to participants. It is also responsible for the preparation of the educational materials that will be used by the children and their families, and for maintaining close surveillance on the health and nutritional status of the children. Finally, support personnel are in charge of cleaning, cooking, and washing.

Planning

In 1975, following the enactment of Law 27, ICBF Regional Offices were required to identify areas in which CAIPs would be located. No prescribed model was provided, nor did any personnel have previous experience with program development. Planning strategies were developed, therefore, on the basis of the criteria spelled out within the law for determining beneficiaries. In Antioquia these strategies were developed for both the municipality of Medellin and the overall department (Villegas and Gonzales, 1975).

As previously indicated, a decision was made at the outset to capitalize on available preschool centers, thereby providing a head start for the program and a savings in money and effort. This strategy also took advantage of the experience of institutions and individuals who had worked with young children. Three other criteria were used to determine the location of the centers: family income, population density, and availability of transportation. Areas were to be selected in which there were a relatively large number of families with incomes less than 2,200 Colombian pesos ($64). Among the first areas identified were those with relatively high rates of unemployment, underemployment, and manual labor, generally on the periphery of the city, and those in which population concentration exceeded 100 or 150 households. At the time the program was implemented, it was clear that the focus was on the most deprived members of the community. If there was concern for making services available to children of public and private employees, it was not immediately apparent. By 1977, however, interest had shifted towards the children of the employed.

Once the areas of greatest need were determined, the next step was to identify all operational preschool centers. These included nursery schools, day care centers, and any other institutions which provided care for children (including health centers). This census led to the identification of: (1) 25 health centers operated by the Ministry of Health, (2) 16 day care centers for custodial care, (3) 21 nursery schools, and (4) 3 community centers.

Following this initial step, ICBF decided to make contractual arrangements with the majority of the organizations which operated these centers, thus providing children with integrated attention as defined by the central office. ICBF also decided to increase their total coverage by creating 53 new centers. In essence, this planning strategy was carried out not only for Medellin, but for the whole region of Antioquia. As of 1977 there were 112 CAIPs in operation throughout Antioquia; 10 were centers for infants and toddlers, and 49 were nursery schools.

As of January 1978 ICBF plans for Antioquia were to focus on improving the services they were already delivering. Although coverage is relatively small in comparison to the number of children who may need services, there were no plans to create new CAIPs. Concerns in terms of future service involve concentration on services for children of employees, particularly in those sections of Antioquia where employers are making contributions to the budget of Public Law 27.

Mode of Operation

Although ICBF may not intend it as policy, there are wide variations among CAIPs in their modes of operation. Large noticeable differences exist in the ages of the children served, the services provided, parental participation, the nature of staff-children interaction, and hygiene and physical facilities.

The CAIPs are intended to serve preschool children from infancy to six years of age. For this purpose the program is subdivided according to the developmental stages of the children. To a certain extent, staff and physical facilities are also arranged accordingly. In the largest CAIPs the breakdown includes a nursery for infants to approximately 24 months, a toddler section from 24 to approximately 36-42 months, a kindergarten, and a transition section for older children.

The program is a departure from the traditional approach, which focused on developing reading and writing skills and following structured schedules and activities, and allowed little time for spontaneity or creativity. In the CAIPs the staff attempts to foster individuality as well as group collaborative behavior. The children have an opportunity to express themselves through play, and idiosyncrasies are reinforced rather than inhibited. There is an attempt to avoid structuring their activities and to encourage projects in which as many children as possible can participate. A particular project, such as the building of a large toy airplane, represents both a game and a collaborative endeavor. The CAIPs also attempt to develop the children's interests in the physical, biological, and social components of their environment. For this purpose the staff builds specific "contents" of varied subject matters, in different corners of the room. Zoological exhibits, botanical corners, or architectural designs may decorate certain room areas where the children spend some portion of their time.

Staff members in the CAIPs have manuals of activities designed to foster the psychomotor development of young children. These manuals present very specific prescriptions for activities to be carried out with infants at different time periods in the first 24 months of age. The activities prescribed, however, are not based on any experimental data that illustrate their effectiveness.

The children at the CAIPs receive three meals a day, five days a week. A menu is prepared following the recommendations of the dietitian at the central office. Daily diets are sufficient to meet the physiological requirements for adequate growth, given the ages of the children. It is not uncommon to encounter recent enrollees in the CAIP program who are in the second or even third stage of malnutrition. The centers do not have the technical or physical facilities to provide specialized dietary services, and undernourished children receive the same diets as those who are well-nourished.

By January 1978 a few CAIPs had made special arrangements for access to pediatric services. The majority of the centers, however, did not have medical support because bureaucratic and political negotiations with municipal health systems had not been completed. When those arrangements are finalized the children will be provided with periodic medical examinations.

A few CAIPs have achieved systematic parental involvement in the organization and function of the centers. ACAIPA has been particularly successful in attracting parental participation, but a great deal remains to be done in order to actively involve parents in other CAIPs.

Thirteen CAIPs in Medellin and Antioquia were visited in January 1978. The objective was to observe the operations of these centers and assess the extent to which they met the written objectives set by ICBF. Perhaps the most prominent features observed during these visits were the degree of organization of the centers, and the heterogeneity of the populations serviced. Children who attend the CAIPs vary from well-groomed, well-dressed, healthy, happy-looking children with rosy cheeks to short-statured, underweight, hypoactive, undernourished-looking children with apathetic physiognomy. These differences go hand-in-hand with the location of the CAIPs. In some sections (for example, Caldas, Ayvra) there were CAIPs (Michin, for example) which could be used as demonstration centers anywhere in the world. Michin was a model of efficiency, cleanliness, and adequate care. The center was spacious with large rooms used only for play and entertainment. There were 60 preschoolers (no infants or toddlers) and the staff:child ratio was approximately 1:8. An interview with the director of the CAIP made it clear that the staff tried to follow closely the philosophy of integrated attention. Once or twice a week parents of the children attended conferences on selected aspects of child care and development.

In other sections of the municipality (San Vicente, for example) some of the CAIPs visited did not appear to differ from custodial care centers in other South American squatter settlements. In one specific case, not only was the director absent during the visit, but neither the staff:child ratio (1:17) nor the physical space were sufficient to provide adequate care for enrolled children. This locale was not well cleaned, and some of the children who looked undernourished had a scent of urine. It was difficult to imagine that these environmental conditions and the overworked staff could serve as a basis for implementation of the philosophy advocated by the CAIP integrated attention program.

It is most important to recognize that ICBF is not directly responsible for the operation of all CAIPs. In some cases, as previously indicated, ICBF has contracted with special agencies or groups to operate certain centers. A few of these agencies have experience in the implementation of programs and the administration of preschool centers, and their operations tend to be carried out with optimal effectiveness. In other cases the administrative agency or group is far less successful and may jeopardize the function of one or more centers. For example, inadequate cost control may result in inefficient, ineffective use of monies in the CAIPs for which the agencies are responsible. Observed differences among CAIPs in their degrees of effectiveness are related to operational differences among administrative agencies. It may be, for example, that a small staff in a particular CAIP is the result of inadequate financial administration on the part of the responsible agency.

Observation determined that in very low-income areas, where unemployment is high and families live as squatters, parents and ICBF staff do not collaborate with any degree of regularity. In some cases the neighborhood has little, if any, input into the planning, implementation, and current activity of the center. This would create no problem if parents were satisfied with the operation, but such is not always the case. In one instance the observer talked at length with two women who were responsible for a parent-community organization. They expressed concern and bitterness because they had no input into the CAIP and complained that although those in the community wanted the CAIP to remain where it was, plans were to move it to another location.

Another distinguishing feature of the CAIPs is the discrepancy between programs for, and treatment of, infants and preschoolers. Although differences exist among CAIPs in the quality of their work with preschoolers, the staff in all of them know what is expected in terms of their work with children. They have received training and instruction in "integrated" work with the three to six year-old child, how activities should be organized around "projects," or how to foster the spontaneity of the children.

In the case of infants, the work is far from clearly set out, especially for the staff. As previously indicated, there is a handbook for psychomotor stimulation, prepared by ICBF, which is to be used by personnel working with infants. The manual only prescribes discrete activities, however, and these can become routinized. It does not discuss the emotional and cognitive needs and demands of the child. The staff is not oriented in setting up activities or in influencing conditions which foster spontaneity, verbal development, or general cognitive growth. Nor are there satisfactory physical arrangements in the rooms where the infants spend a good part of the day. In the centers visited the cribs were placed side by side with only a few centimeters between them, and gave the distinct impression of being overcrowded. In general, arrangements for infants were of a custodial nature. It is not surprising that planning for CAIPs has focused on the older rather than on the younger child.

CONCLUSIONS

In November 1977 in Antioquia and Medellin enrollment in CAIPs and other preschool centers operating under the aegis of ICBF totaled 10,862 children, 2,480 fewer than the enrollment approved by ICBF. Ideal enrollment (13,242) represents approximately 10 percent of the 132,389 children from households with no fixed incomes, with incomes under 2,200 pesos ($64) per month, or who live in squatter settlements. The percentage of coverage within this population is extremely small in light of the fact that an important philosophical aim of the program is to protect the development of children who live in poverty. The situation becomes even more critical when children of both public and private employers, legal candidates for the CAIPs, are added to the eligible population. The total is thus raised to nearly 200,000 children.

The CAIP program appears to prevent developmental derangements among infants who join the program early in life and to ameliorate the adverse effects of poverty among those enrolled during preschool years. Even if the Colombian government is committed to mounting the program on a national scale, however, there are serious questions about its ability to finance an operation of this magnitude. Using the most recent figures available for expenditures and population coverage in Antioquia, it can be estimated that the cost of providing CAIPs to the 100,000 children who are in great need of the program may come to $100,000,000 for this department alone.

Perhaps the essential problem with the CAIPs is that not all of them fulfill the objectives for which they were created. Some appear to function as centers for custodial care rather than as centers for the prevention or improvement of derangements in growth and development. Cost effectiveness analyses carried out for this program must take these facts into account. The question then becomes whether the expenditure of such substantial sums can be justified for what amounts to custodial care.

7

CASE STUDY 2:
PUNO, PERU

The Initial Education program was begun in 1972 as part of the educational reform in Peru (Drysdale and Myers, 1975). It began as a public intervention program that constituted the first level of Peru's National Education System. The goals of the program are: (1) to assure that the basic physical and mental needs of children 0–5 years of age are met through programs of educational intervention and "nutritional and social complementation," and by improving the ability of parents to meet these needs; (2) to enable parents and communities to reorganize and mobilize community resources on behalf of young children; and (3) to serve as a vehicle for detection and treatment of developmental problems in young children (Ministerio de Educacion/Peru, 1972, Article 79).

The target populations for the program are children from rural and marginally urban areas whose environments fail to provide basic developmental needs. Up to the present time Initial Education has been center-based and has used formal kindergarten centers and primary school classrooms as the basis for program functions. The program is essentially educational; nutrition and health components are minimal in all but a few of the centers.

This chapter focuses on PROPEDEINE, the Non-Formal Early Childhood Education Project in Puno. This early intervention program, whose goal is to help meet the developmental needs of young children in Peru's rural zone, uses paraprofessional teachers (promotores) from the participating communities, and focuses on the provision of educational services to children from three to five years of age. Nutritional supplementation and health control are also provided as secondary services.

The program currently operates in six of nine provinces in the department of Puno and reaches approximately 5,000 (3 percent) of the 168,000 children in the 0-5 year age group. There are 144 centers now in operation, and current plans include opening centers in the three provinces farthest from the town of Puno. The majority of enrollees are 3-5 years of age. Before describing this program in detail, it will be useful to consider the aspects of poverty in Peru and, specifically, in Puno.

DEMOGRAPHIC TRENDS

Peru's population of 16 million is the fourth largest in South America and, depending on the region considered (Sewell, 1977), is growing at an annual rate of 3.0 to 3.4 percent. Given moderately declining fertility, the population will reach approximately 34 million by the end of the century (Gall, 1974). Twenty percent or 3.2 million are children under five years of age. Even given the same declining fertility rate, predictions are that by the year 2000 there will be 6.4 million children under six years of age (Gall, 1974) (see also Table 4, Chapter 1). While the expanding population may not be excessive in terms of available land, it is excessive in terms of per capita productivity (Weil, 1972).

One-half of Peru's population is Mestizo (descendants of Spanish and Indian), one-third is Indian, and one-seventh is Spanish. Approximately 50 percent of the population lives in the coastal region, 42.5 percent inhabit the Sierra, and 7.5 percent live in the jungle (Van den Berghe and Primov, 1977).

Like Colombia, Peru is undergoing rapid urbanization, and urban habitants make up 63.5 percent of the total population. As of 1970 an estimated 100,000 persons per year migrated to Lima, resulting in a growth rate of approximately 5.88 percent. Between 1961 and 1972 the population of metropolitan Lima increased by 83 percent (USAID/Peru, 1975), and by 1974 the estimated population was 3,200,000. By comparison, Arequipa, the second largest city in the country, probably has a population no greater than 350,000 (Oficina Nacional de Estadistica y Censo, 1974).

As a consequence of this urbanization, squatter settlements and slums make up a large sector of the city and surrounding areas. These over-populated, low-income areas often have no electricity or potable water, and medical or social services are either unavailable or extremely rare. Burton suggests that El Salvador, one of the shanty towns which form a belt around the metropolitan area, may have as many as 200,000 inhabitants. He notes that the average family consists of two adults and six or seven children, that only 25 percent of adult males have regular employment, and that the average industrial wage is $2 to $3 per day (Burton, 1976).

SOCIOECONOMIC CHARACTERISTICS

The extreme inequality which characterizes Peru's internal economy is illustrated by the recently estimated 49:1 ratio between top and bottom deciles in the distribution of total income (for detailed discussion of income distribution in Peru, see Webb, 1975; Webb and Figueroa, 1975). From 1961 until the present it has been estimated that the top 1 percent of the population received 49.2 percent of total income while the bottom 20 percent received only 2.5 percent. This level of inequality ranks among the most severe in the world (Webb, 1975).

The dominance of the Spanish and Mestizo populations over the Indians has been historically (Mariategui, 1971), and continues to be, the central social and economic characteristic of Peruvian life (Lowenthal, 1975; Van den Berghe and Primov, 1977). This dominance has been manifested in socioeconomic exploitation of the Indian on large agricultural estates; political neglect of the Sierra, where the majority of the Indian population lives; and the dominance of coastal values (Handelman, 1975; Cotler, 1975; Van den Berghe and Primov, 1977). The exploitation of the Indian is illustrated by the radically uneven income distribution between the city of Lima, with its mean annual income of $870, and the five contiguous Indian-populated departments of Apurimac, Ayacucho, Cuzco, Huancavelica, and Puno with their average yearly income of $280 (Webb, 1975). In political terms, the neglect of the Sierra has meant a lack of social services. Urban areas, for example, have approximately 14.5 physicians per 10,000 inhabitants, and thus fare better than rural areas which have as few as 1.6 physicians per 10,000 population (UNICEF, 1973, 1975; Van den Berghe and Primov, 1977).

Studying the socioeconomic characteristics of families in low-income areas, on a micro level, clearly illustrates the difficult social environment encountered by the children. Frisancho, Klayman, and Matos (1976) assessed the reproductive, anthropometric, and socioeconomic characteristics of 4,952 mothers and their newborns. The sample was taken from the Maternidad de Lima, a public hospital which serves primarily a low-income population, the majority of which has migrated to the city from provinces outside the department of Lima. The mean number of school years completed for the fathers and mothers of the newborns were 6.27 and 4.11 years, respectively. Mean per capita income was $229 and per capita food expense was $144, or more than 50 percent of total income. Conceptions averaged 3.65 and live offsprings 3.06. A significant negative covariation existed between socioeconomic status and number of births. These infants, then, were born to low-income, poorly educated parents, into families which were already relatively large, which spent a major portion of total income on food, and which exhibited relatively high probabilities for early mortality.

In another study, Pollitt and Ricciuti (1969) investigated the socioeconomic background of 90 preschoolers in the slums of Lima. The sample, drawn from day care center enrollment records in slum areas, appears to be more deprived economically than the sample used by Frisancho, Layman, and Matos (1976). Thus, the mean years of education for mothers of this group was not more than 2.0 years, approximately 55 percent of mothers were functionally illiterate, the reported monthly income was about $50, and the family size averaged between six and seven people.

It is important to note that Peru is varied geographically, socioeconomically, and socioculturally, and that no description adequately represents the situation of infants and young children.

NUTRITION AND HEALTH

In 1973 it was noted that in spite of an upward trend in net availability of food, Peru was still far below the recommended dietary allowances of the Food and Agriculture Organization of the United Nations, especially those for protein and energy (Comision Multisectorial del Plan Nacional de Politica Alimentaria y Nutricional, 1973). In the coastal area the mean calorie and protein intakes for both rural and urban communities were 2,068 and 50.6 grams and represented a 17 and 22 percent deficit, respectively. Many families in the mountain region had intakes which were less than 75 percent of recommendations. In some sections in the Amazon region nearly 95 percent of children included in various nutrition surveys were found to have a generally deficient nutrient intake.

The health of young children in Peru is inadequate by most of the epidemiological standards used for international comparisons. Infant mortality rate, by recent estimates, is over 130 per 1,000 live births (UNICEF/CEPAL, 1979). Peru's mortality rate for young children is the third highest in the Americas and is associated with a high prevalence of enteritis and diarrheal diseases resulting from gastrointestinal infection; pneumonia, influenza, and other respiratory infections; and protein-energy malnutrition, avitaminosis, and other nutritional deficiencies. Patterns of morbidity are similar, with respiratory diseases exceeding gastrointestinal infection as a serious health threat in certain regions of the Sierra (PAHO, 1974a). A large-scale study, conducted at the Children's Hospital in Lima from 1957 to 1974 on 327,131 patients showed that 35.5 percent were hospitalized with acute diarrhea as a primary symptom and 67 percent were hospitalized with some degree

of undernutrition (Comision Multisectorial del Plan Nacional de Politica Alimentaria y Nutricional, 1973).

In 1971 only 391 maternal and child health centers existed
and they attended only 26.5 percent of births. Many of the remaining
73.5 percent of pregnant women were assisted in their homes by informally trained midwives or "knowledgeable" relatives (UNICEF,
1973). Despite the fact that children under 11 years of age make up
one-third of Peru's population, only an estimated 9 percent of hospital
beds are set aside for pediatrics (Gall, 1974; UNICEF, 1973).

This lack of emphasis on the health needs of pregnant and
nursing women and young children has been noted by health professionals and organizations operating within Peru (Burton, 1976;
UNICEF, 1973, 1975). It appears to be a widespread phenomenon
in developing countries.

EDUCATION

Enrollment in primary school has increased steadily over
the past 20 years. In 1950, for example, enrollment was 1,010,200;
by 1962 it had risen to 2,759,600. A comparison of school expenditures as a percentage of GNP also shows a clear upward trend. Between 1951 and 1971 educational expenditures increased from 1.6 to
4.5 percent of GNP, and projections were that the latter rate would
be maintained over the following four years (Drysdale and Myers,
1975). Despite these favorable changes, however, it was still apparent in 1977 that services continued to be concentrated in urban
areas or in rural zones with already well-developed infrastructures,
and that services were unavailable to those children in most need of
them (Halpern, 1977).

The citation from R. C. Castillo (1975) in Chapter 2 illustrates
the qualitative characteristics of the educational system in Peru, especially as they relate to low-income children. In this context it is
not surprising that the primary school drop out rate grows appreci-
ably from year to year. Data for primary and basic regular enrollment for 1974 in the public school system show that 630,261 children
were enrolled in first grade. The figure dropped to 413,963 for the
third grade, and 234,056 for the sixth (USAID/Peru, 1975).

There is also a markedly uneven rural-urban distribution
among school enrollees. Data for 1975 show that of 178,600 children
enrolled in preschool programs, 86.3 percent were urban residents.
In primary and secondary school there were 2,449,837 and 824,661
enrollees, respectively, and 61.9 percent and 91.8 percent were
urban residents (USAID/Peru, 1975).

In 1969 the new military government appointed an Educational Reform Commission whose mandate was to reorganize the educational system of Peru. The aim of the Commission was to adapt the educational process to the country's economic and social development needs, and a General Education Law was promulgated in 1972. Among the highlights of the law was a new emphasis on the needs of Peru's infants and children. A program, called Initial Education (IE) was thus established within the educational system to meet those needs.

This program for infants and young children, as conceptualized, would employ a number of strategies to reach parents and children. The existing formal kindergarten center infrastructure would be incorporated into the program, and in rural communities emphasis would be placed on the development of nonformal programs for young children and parents.

Three broad categories were formed within the Initial Education program: Centers of Initial Education, nonformal programs for children 3 to 5 years of age, and nonformal programs involving families and communities. Two types of formal programs are included within the Centers of Initial Education: "cunas" for children 0-3 years of age, and "jardines" for those from 3 to 5. In addition, some formal center programs have incorporated nonformal programs, particularly activities designed for parents and communities.

As originally conceived, the thrust of IE's effort was toward children 0-6 years of age living in marginal urban zones and "frontier zones" (communities far from administrative centers and often near Peru's borders). Generally, these were jungle and sierra regions where there was little or no social sector infrastructure. In areas of insufficient population concentration, the nonformal program was to be the chief vehicle for provision of services.

According to program documents (Ministerio de Educacion/ Peru, 1975, 1976), nonformal programs for parents can have varied focuses: food production, family life planning, recreation, crafts, social mobilization, paraprofessional training, education and agrarian reforms, child-rearing techniques, early stimulation in the home, and feeding of children under six. Nonformal programs for children 3-5 years of age are expected to contain elements of psychoeducational stimulation, nutrition, and basic health.

Formal, center-based programs for children from 3 to 5 are the most numerous by far (Ministerio de Educacion/Peru, 1976). The number of children in the 0-3 age range served by formaul "cunas" is negligible and amounts to barely 1 percent of the total population served by the program. Both technical and financial considerations play a part in the neglect of this group. The technical reasons include insufficient knowledge concerning development and operation of infant centers, educational and physical needs of infants and toddlers, and the training required to ensure competent staff. Financial reasons include the higher per capita cost in the 0-3 age group that results from the necessity of maintaining a lower staff-child ratio and higher physical plant costs.

The Initial Education program was designed to work closely with the health and nutrition sectors to provide various services to young children and families through IE centers, health clinics, and maternal and child care centers. The activities were designed to be complementary rather than integrated; thus IE programs would not run in health clinics or vice versa. Although IE centers are sometimes used for immunizations, medical examinations, and other health control activities, and food supplements for young children are used for IE's lunch program, to date there have been no joint programs.

Principal forms of cooperation with respect to personnel have involved in-service seminars designed to increase staff knowledge in the areas of basic nutrition and health. Ministry staff also provide lectures on these topics for parents of children attending IE programs. Coordination of activities, when it occurs, tends to be at the community level.

In 1978 IE formal education programs were reaching approximately 6 percent (191,123) of the population in the 0-5 age group. Regional coverage varies from as low as 2.8 percent in the southern Sierra to 8 percent in selected coastal areas. As previously indicated, only about 1 percent of young children enrolled in the program are in the 0-3 age group.

IE's annual growth rate, in terms of coverage of the 0-5 population group, has been approximately 21 percent annually for the past few years. During the same period, enrollment in IE as a percentage of enrollment in the educational system has increased from 3.3 to 4 percent and the teaching force has increased by 22 percent thereby matching enrollment growth (1,400 children are born daily). The program has not increased its proportional coverage.

In nutrition and health areas the program has been inhibited by lack of technical knowledge on the part of the IE staff, and by practical and political problems which impede fuller intersectoral coordination. In addition, IE is reaching children only when they are three, four, or five years of age. Most importantly, perhaps, since they have the greatest influence on the child's nutritional and health status, IE has been reaching parents only in the most marginal way (group discussions, for example).

Observations in various settings, and data on the intra- and interregional distribution of IE activities (Ministerio de Educacion/

Peru, 1976), suggest that the program has not been reaching that portion of the population which lives in the greatest poverty and exhibits the greatest lack of social services. Within the framework of historical distribution of early childhood services, IE has been relatively successful in redistributing services to populations in need of them, but the unwillingness or inability of IE's leadership to support new strategies for provision of services (nonformal and home-based programs) has inhibited the program's ability to reach young children and families in rural and marginal urban zones.

It appears that IE's attempts to bring about redistribution of services by devoting increased resources to nonformal programs, have not been entirely successful. The population which has benefitted from these attempts is a subgroup of the total population which, though poor, has already benefitted from the social reforms of the early 1970s. This process has been described by Cotler (1975) as "segmentary redistribution." Children and families living in the greatest poverty, particularly those in rural zones of the southern Sierra, remain almost totally out of reach of the program.

THE PUNO SETTING

Puno is located in southeastern Peru and borders Bolivia on the east; the departments of Madre de Dios and Cuzco on the west; and Arequipa, Moquegua, and Tacna on the south. It is the fourth largest of Peru's departments and most of its area lies in the Sierra region. Lake Titicaca, the world's highest navigable waterway, intrudes into the department from the east and jurisdiction over the lake is shared with Bolivia (Dew, 1969; Handelman, 1975). Altitude varies from 300 to 6,000 meters within the department and the ecology ranges from subtropical in the north to alpine in the Andean region. The altiplano, the predominant ecological zone, covers 40 percent of the total area and ranges in elevation from 3,600 to 5,000 meters. The snowline is at 15,000 feet.

Puno is among the most populous regions in Peru; it is surpassed only by Lima, Cajamarca, and Piura. According to the 1972 census, its population of 813,172 represented 5.8 percent of the national total. Fifty-three percent of Puno's population is under 20 years of age, and only 3.7 percent is over 65 years of age. Approximately 168,000 persons, 20 percent of the population, are five years of age or younger.

Seventy-six percent of Puno's population is rural and 24 percent is urban. The majority of the population is concentrated around Lake Titicaca and near the major rivers. There are seven communities with more than 5,000 inhabitants and two towns, Puno and

Juliaca, with approximately 50,000 inhabitants each. In spite of rural migration to Puno and Juliaca, the general population of the department increased only 1 percent annually between 1940 and 1972. The migration from Puno to other areas of the Sierra and to Peru's coastal region accounts for the low overall increase. The effect of Puno's population distribution has been to create better organized rural communities in selected settings, in terms of political and economic infrastructure, and to concentrate social services in population clusters.

Most agricultural activity is of the subsistence type. Key crops are several varieties of potato, barley, coffee, and a local grain called quinua. Cocoa and wheat are also cultivated, cattle are raised for both meat and dairy products, and sheep, llama, alpacas, and vicunas are raised for wool. The risks inherent in Puno's ecological setting make it difficult for small farmers to obtain the loans necessary to make improvements in their agricultural practices (Millikan and Hapgood, 1967).

The marketing of agricultural products is hampered by transportation difficulties between rural areas and more populous zones. Although the flatness of the altiplano has made the construction of roads relatively easy, regular flooding during the rainy season makes them impassable during much of the year. There are railroads to the major cities of Arequipa and Cuzco but, because of the inadequate transportation facilities, farmers are unable to get their products to the rail centers in Juliaca and Puno.

Approximately 55 percent of the population speaks Quechua and 40 percent speaks Aymara. Native Spanish-speaking residents are outnumbered about 20 to 1; an estimated 8 percent of Puno's adult population speaks little or no Spanish (Handelman, 1975; Dew, 1969). Bilingualism is increasing, however, because the Quechua and Aymara languages are not similar enough to be mutually understood and communications between the groups are usually conducted in Spanish.

The health situation in Puno can best be described in statistical terms. In Lima the ratio of physicians to inhabitants is approximately 1:700, while in Puno it is 1:12,000. Health services exist in only 45.2 percent of the geographical area of the department. The 5 hospitals, 14 health centers, and 73 health stations, all "inadequately equipped," amount to one health establishment for every 8,695 inhabitants. There are .54 physicians, 146 nurses, and .13 health technicians for every 10,000 residents (UNICEF, 1973, 1975).

There has been little research into the nutritional status of the population. Picon-Reategui (1976) reviewed studies of food habits and nutritional status in one rural district of Puno and reports that both have been changing in response to improved access to Juliaca and Puno. In 1964 tubers were identified as the staple food, and they provided 74.2 percent of total caloric intake. By 1969, however, cereals were identified as the staple, and the source of this change was identified as increased access to food from the United States.

Protein and calorie intake in the district surveyed by Picon-Reategui was found to be adequate for all but pregnant and nursing women, and children from birth to one year of age (1976). Protein consumption was inadequate for children under three years of age and Vitamin A intake was notably low for the population as a whole.

A report on the general nutrition situation in Puno cites the average daily protein consumption as 55 grams, 3 percent of which is of animal origin (UNICEF, 1975). A World Health Organization study (1971) places the prevalence of severe and moderate protein calorie malnutrition at 5 percent, and of moderate protein calorie malnutrition at 4.4 percent of the one-to-four age group.

PROPEDEINE: PUNO NON-FORMAL EARLY CHILDHOOD EDUCATION PROJECT

In 1965 a group of Peruvian professionals, working in various social sector programs in the department of Puno, organized a parent education program in nutrition and health for rural campesino (peasant) mothers in the region. The women were to receive basic knowledge and skills necessary for better fulfillment of their children's developmental needs. The team was composed of anthropologists, social workers, teachers, and university students, all of whom were seeking ways to attack the persistent social deprivation and poverty found throughout the department. They identified mothers and young children as the most deprived segments of the population, and the meeting of their needs as the key to social development.

Mothers brought their children to class and the project soon developed a child care and supplementary feeding component, which gradually became the main focus of the program. Food was donated by CARITAS (a Catholic social welfare agency) and USAID. The mothers took turns preparing lunch and received basic knowledge related to nutrition and food preparation. As the program grew, officials from Puno's private early childhood program began to take an interest. In 1968 volunteers from the Escuela Normal in Puno, who had completed academic studies in early childhood education, began doing their internships in some of the rural communities in the department. With assistance from CARITAS, child care centers to house early childhood activity programs were constructed in the rural communities already involved.

Early in 1968 the Ministry of Education began to assign regular teachers to the program. An evaluation conducted later that year (PROPEDEINE, 1976) concluded that local volunteers, young campesinos from the communities involved, were the most effective teachers in the centers, and that professional educators were more valuable in supervisory roles. Thus began the use of community-selected, community-raised paraprofessionals as teachers in the program. In 1973 the program came under the jurisdiction of the Ministry of Education and what was then the Direccion General de Educacion Inicial y Basica Regular. The Ministry provided technical assistance and limited funds, but the majority of funding, principally for training of paraprofessionals and supervision of activities, came from UNICEF.

The current status of the project is problematical. Local and national Initial Education officials view it as logically falling under their jurisdiction, while the PROPEDEINE administrative and technical support team view the project as a unique experiment in community-based and community-generated educational activity that, in their words, would be "destroyed" by the bureaucratic mechanisms of the Ministry. The project's continued autonomy is thus in doubt, although previous attempts to incorporate it into the regular system have failed.

Program Philosophy and Objectives

PROPEDEINE was developed generally in response to locally perceived needs of young children and families. The philosophy is that social intervention efforts must be generated from within the socioeconomic, political, and cultural realities of a target population, and must yield to these realities as planning and theory are translated into practice.

In 1976 the objective was stated as follows:

To contribute to the development of the rural population of the Department of Puno by inducing the generation of maximal educational opportunities through satisfaction of the minimal essential learning and developmental needs of campesino children 0-6 years of age. At the same time, to provide the campesino child with the learning skills to take maximum advantage of learning opportunities in whatever setting he finds himself (PROPEDEINE, 1976, p. 10).

The project is an attempt to meet basic physical needs while developing cognitive and other psychosocial abilities conducive to success in subsequent schooling. The strategy is to mobilize the rural community to accept responsibility for day-to-day intervention activities, while providing technical support from a team of professionals thoroughly familiar with the communities involved. The communities choose both the location of the center and the community member to be trained as teacher (the promotor), build the center, and supervise day-to-day activities. The PROPEDEINE team provides technical support, gives the program direction, and acts as a buffer between the communities involved and bureaucratic social development mechanisms. A secondary objective of the project is to raise the consciousness of rural communities concerning the importance of meeting young children's needs, and to place and keep responsibility within the family. It is an attempt to support the family by making it a conscious educational vehicle.

Organization and Administration

The program includes the promotores (paraprofessional teachers), the PROPEDEINE team, and community members. The promotores are chosen from the community and are usually men in their twenties who have had either a complete primary education or a primary and some secondary education. They serve as formal center teachers and community-level program administrators for PROPEDEINE. They are selected by influential community members, chosen either formally or informally to decide on community issues.

Training for promotores requires approximately two months and consists of: an introduction to elementary child-development concepts; familiarization with the organization, activities, and curriculum developed by PROPEDEINE; and some practical work with children. The child-development component is based on Piagetian development theory; it is also claimed that the curriculum follows an early intervention model developed by the High/Scope Educational Research Foundation of Ypsilanti, Michigan.

Halpern (1977) found, through interviews with the promotores and through observation of their interaction with the children, that they have a great deal of pride in themselves and in their work, and that they enjoy their occupation. He also noted, as did Llanos and Flores (1976), that they felt constrained by a lack of understanding on the part of fellow community members about the purpose of the promotores' activities, by a lack of learning materials, and by

inadequate support from the PROPEDEINE team. They are also in
an insecure economic position that involves working for long periods
of time with no salary.

The PROPEDEINE team provides technical and administrative
support for the project. Administratively it operates in a horizontal
fashion, with no hierarchy, and responsibilities revolve around tasks
and geographic zones. The team consists of four early childhood
educators, and other specialists in various areas of education,
anthropology, and community development. Most have worked for
a number of years in the department of Puno, and some have been
with the project since its inception in 1965 as a parent education
program. All team members speak either Quechua or Aymara.

The third major provider in the PROPEDEINE project is the
community. Its participation in all activities, except training, has
been the key to the survival and growth of the PROPEDEINE project.
In remote rural highland areas it would be all but impossible to run
this type of program without full and active community support. The
community not only builds and maintains the centers, but cooks the
meals, supplies the food in some cases, helps support the promotor
economically, makes some of the educational material, decides on
center policy, and generally provides the resources for the center's
survival.

The principal activity of the project is the creation of an early
childhood education center, called a Wawa Wasi in Quechua and a
Wawa Uta in Aymara, that provides educational and nutritional supplementation programs for children from three to five years of age.
There are 144 centers in rural communities around the department.
Unfortunately, the center-based nature of the program, the special
training needed, and the lack of adequate facilities discourage the
provision of formal center services for the 0 to 3 age group.

Along with the program for children, the centers provide a
focal point for other PROPEDEINE-related activities such as parent
meetings, visits by local health officials, and general community
assemblies. While there are few formal parent education activities,
parents do observe the promotores working with the children and may
learn new modes of interacting with their children through these observations.

A second activity of the project is the home-based psychoeducational stimulation program. For this activity a young campesino
woman from the community, if possible one having four or five years
of primary education, is trained as a home visitor. She works with
mothers from her community on such issues as stimulation of the 0-2
year old infant, nutrition and food preparation and basic hygiene.
She is chosen by the community, and thus has access to home situations. The hours of visitation and the approach taken are carefully

chosen, taking into account the economic and cultural limitations on such activity (for example, work patterns in the fields).

Another component of the project is the use of mass media, principally radio, as a vehicle for parent education activities and also as a means of continually updating the knowledge of promotores. The author was unable to determine how widespread the use of radio has been in the project or what the contents of the radio messages are, and no data are available on who is receiving and using radio information.

Curriculum and Learning Activities

Halpern (1977) was also informed by a High/Scope Foundation visitor to the project that the curriculum guide had been translated into Spanish, with very little adaptation, and that it serves as the basic document for promotor training. No systematically collected data are available on the effect of using the High/Scope curriculum, developed in the U.S., in the distinctive cultural and environmental setting that exists in Puno. The lack of evaluation and analysis of this transfer is critical not only in terms of the effect on Puno children, but also because the present use may suggest a degree of success not actually achieved.

The language of instruction in the Wawa Wasi/Utas is Quechua or Aymara. However, the promotores do introduce Spanish words and concepts as part of many group lessons. This setting exerts less pressure than a first grade classroom.

Educational materials available in the Wawa Wasi/Utas are scarce by European and American standards, but remarkable by the standards of the communities in which they are found. There are locally made toys, games, dolls, and puzzles, and "imported" materials, generally donated by UNICEF. Promotores and others involved in the program, however, recognize the scarcity of learning materials and state that their ability to implement educational activities is adversely effected as a result (Llanos and Flores, 1976). The degree of scarcity tends to vary with the initiative of the promotor.

Most centers are made of locally derived materials (stone, adobe bricks, matting, and so forth) but some have concrete or wood portions. Local materials are provided by the communities involved, while cement and corrugated roofing are usually donated by CARITAS and UNICEF. Construction labor is volunteered by community members. Most materials and facilities inside the center are hand-made, though some centers have desks, chairs, or toys provided by the donor agencies. Nearly all Wawa Wasi/Utas have outhouses or latrines at a suitable distance from the building itself. A few centers

have outdoor play equipment, generally constructed of wood by community members, and some also have gardens for children to cultivate.

Within the centers, simple walls are used to differentiate the
four principal activity areas: house, art, silence, and workshop.
These areas are developed around the learning center concept, common to early childhood education programs throughout the world. In
each area simple wooden or cardboard shelves and boxes hold toys,
games, puzzles, and other learning materials. In the center of each
Wawa Wasi/Uta is a group activity area, in which the children's
chairs are usually located.

PROPEDEINE has had a supplementary feeding component
since its inception, with most foods donated by CARITAS, and some
by USAID. Lately, the level of these donations has been low, and
parents often bring their own food to the centers and cook lunch for
the children. Direct observation reveals that lunches include mostly
potatoes, bread, or some other grain, in combination with a few
vegetables and meat. In the past the supplementary food program
was a "drawing" device; parents would send their children to the
centers for the purpose of receiving the free lunch. It is now obvious,
however, that the feeding component has not been guided by considerations of nutritional adequacy. Moreover, no special efforts have
been made to develop meals rich in nutrients scarce to the region,
or to use the supplementary feeding as an educational component for
parents.

Evaluations Conducted to Date

In October/November 1976 Llanos and Flores, two Peruvian
professionals, conducted a formal evaluation of the activities of the
Wawa Wasi/Utas. This evaluation was funded by the U.S. Agency
for International Development. Fisk, Adams, and Evans (1977) also
conducted an informal evaluation in September 1976 as a part of a
consultancy for USAID by the High/Scope Educational Research
Foundation.

Llanos and Flores made observations in 13 Wawa Wasi/Utas,
using two structured questionnaires (one each for parents and promotores), and three psychological tests (Harris-Goodenough draw-a-
figure test for intellectual development, Gesell's schedules of visual-
motor maturity, and Vineland's social maturity scales). These tools
tapped the intellectual development, visual-motor, and social maturity of the children. Sociological data were gathered in a number
of areas: levels and types of parent participation; parent perceptions
of various aspects of the program, including its effect on their children; perceptions of the promotores regarding their roles vis-a-vis

the children and community, their feelings about working with young children, and their analysis of program problems; and the opinions of promotores and parents as to the general effectiveness of the program.

The sample consisted of 13 promotores, 83 parents (62 fathers, 21 mothers), and 234 children 3 years of age (120 male, 114 female) in 13 Wawa Wasi/Utas. Eighty-one percent of the parents, 83 percent of the children, and 77 percent of the promotores were Aymara-speaking. The remainder were Quechua-speaking. Average length of attendance of children from various age groups was as follows: 3-year-olds, 12 months; 4-year-olds, 12 months; 5-year-olds, 15 months; 6-year-olds, 22 months. Eighty-two percent of the parents had a primary education, but 61 percent of mothers were illiterate.

The psychological tests were given to groups of 15-20 children, with instructions in Quechua or Aymara. The questionnaires for parents and promotores were administered individually with a PROPEDEINE team member serving as translator for those (65 percent of the total) who did not speak Spanish. Centers to be visited were selected by the PROPEDEINE team and Llanos and Flores also note that children were given special help by some promotores and PROPEDEINE team members. Promotores were notified in advance of the evaluation team's scheduled visits.

Some of the principal findings of the study were:

1. The three and four-year-olds were found to be within the norms in visual-motor maturity for their age group, while the five and six-year-olds were found to be below normal.

2. The IQ scores, measured by the Harris-Goodenough scale, ranged from 71 for the five-year-olds to 76 for the six-year-olds. No explanation is given for the low scores except to say that the test was not normal for this population.

3. Boys scored higher than girls in all psychological tests.

4. Using a very loose adaptation of Vineland's social maturity scale, the investigators found a high level of social maturity; at an average chronological age of 4.7, social maturity was found to be 5.8.

5. The promotores found all the children to be very strong on group participation; older children were found to be strong in planning activities, hygiene, creativity, and language.

6. The promotores feel pride in their work, and feel that they are making a contribution to the lives of participating children. They also feel constrained by: lack of understanding on the part of the community members about what they are attempting to accomplish; lack of learning materials; inadequate support from the PROPEDEINE team; and the insecurity of their economic situation. The promotores recognize the social significance of the program, that is, the potential long range effects of their activities on the children, and they

feel that PROPEDEINE is "in accord with the reality of the child and his community."

7. Parents felt their children were more "ready"—agile, aggressive, lively—as a result of participation in the program. Some would prefer that the program teach more reading and writing; all felt that the program was benefitting their children.

8. Elementary school teachers in the region found that children who had been involved in the project adapted more easily to the first grade than did nonparticipants.

Llanos' and Flores' overall conclusion is that the approach taken by the project has worked well. The project appears to affect behavioral patterns and cognitive abilities of children positively, and parents were committed to the project; however, due to the obvious methodological limitations (that is, no control group) no conclusive inferences can be drawn.

The High/Scope Educational Research Foundation group (Fisk, Adams, and Evans, 1977) stated in the report of their consultancy that

> The work in Puno is demonstrating that there may be ways that the mobilization of community resources can effectively establish and maintain developmentally appropriate educational experience for preschool age children even in the most isolated, poorest of environments (1977, p. 6).

Their report also mentions a number of problems: the lack of measurable project objectives; the need to develop an alternative promotor training model because, given the magnitude of demand for services and lack of financial resources, the current model is too costly to work on a larger scale; and the need for an easily replicable set of training and promotor support materials. The problems, however, are overshadowed by the evidence indicating that traditional, rural communities can be mobilized around social development concerns.

CONCLUSIONS

Peru's program in Initial Education began as an ambitious undertaking to provide selective educational, health, and nutritional services to the country's preschool population. The original concept focused on the socioeconomically deprived segment of the population. Over time, however, budgetary restraints and other restrictions resulted in a significant decrease, within the Ministry of Education, in the emphasis given to the preschool period. The future of this type of program is unpredictable, but it is clear that the momentum of the early 1970s has been lost.

PROPEDEINE was a most unusual program, in Latin America in general and in Peru in particular. It grew out of the efforts of community members in Puno who had a deep concern for the developmental needs of the young child. A strong organization was initiated in response to this concern and the resulting program appears to be providing beneficial services to infants and preschool children. The program clearly illustrates that preschool intervention programs may rely heavily on the community and may even be used as instruments of social change.

The future of PROPEDEINE is unclear. It is no longer an autonomous organization, but now forms part of the Ministry of Education. It is not apparent yet whether the financial and organizational problems of the Ministry will affect its operation, but the possibility exists. On the other hand, the success of the program has awakened the interest of international organizations and funding agencies, and their backing may provide the financial means for continued operation. It is the hope of those concerned that the nature of the program will not be distorted as its reputation expands.

8
CASE STUDY 3:
CARACAS, VENEZUELA

Recent interest in the development of a young child policy in Venezuela appears to be associated with the rise in national income. New policies have been established as a first step in defining appropriate allocation of the additional funds; however, these policies are general and vague and must be more precisely defined if they are to lead to action (Eskenasy, 1978).

The two previous chapters examined a restricted number of programs in Antioquia, Colombia, and Puno, Peru. This chapter focuses on the large number of programs operative in Caracas, Venezuela. Although the diverse services provided appear to have common goals, the programs lack efficiency and produce limited benefits in spite of enormous cost. Venezuela is financially better off than the majority of South American countries and it might be expected that their poverty programs would be more effective than those of poorer countries. This is not the case, however, and clear similarities exist between operations in Colombia and Peru and what is occurring in Venezuela.

DEMOGRAPHIC TRENDS

Venezuela has a population of 12 million and is growing at an annual rate of 3.5 percent (IDB, 1975). It is estimated that the population will double every 21 years (Osio Sandoval and Medina Colina, 1977). Assuming moderately declining fertility, the population is expected to reach 25 million by the turn of the century. A demographic breakdown by age emphasizes, as in Colombia and Peru, the young population structure: the 2,600,000 children between zero and six years of age represent 21.6 percent of the total population (Fundacion del Nino, 1977). Predictions are that by the end of the century

Venezuela will have 5,250,000 million children under six years of age.

About 65 percent of the population of Venezuela is Mestizo (mixed Indian and European ancestry), 21 percent of European origin (mainly Spanish), 7 percent Negro, 2 percent Indian, and the remainder mulatto or mixed Indian and Negro ancestry. Seventy-five percent of the population is urban and the bulk of it is distributed among six cities in the northern part of the country: Caracas, Maracaibo, Valencia, Barquisieto, Maracay, and San Cristobal.

In addition to high birth rates, immigration is a major contributor to population growth. Fifty-one and a half percent of the internal immigration comes from other Venezuelan urban centers of more than 20,000 inhabitants, and 23.1 percent comes from rural areas of fewer than 5,000 inhabitants. A study of reasons for immigration to Caracas revealed that 40.5 percent comes in search of employment, and 35.9 percent comes for family reasons (Chen, 1970). The same study reports that, upon arrival, 25 percent of these immigrants lives in shacks under poor sanitary conditions and that 10.5 percent of the migrating men and 34.1 percent of the women are unable to find work. The sex difference in employment success is likely to be a result of the lower educational level of the women. By 1977 there were approximately 162,80 shacks in Caracas (Banco Obrero, 1972). Assuming six inhabitants for each (four children, two parents) the projected population was 976,000. Given the 20 percent of the population of Caracas which is of preschool age (MSAS, 1976b), it can be estimated that 195,000, or 3 percent of the preschool population of the city, lives in shacks. In addition, there are many city center preschoolers who live in equally deplorable circumstances.

SOCIOECONOMIC CONDITIONS

National per capita income in 1975 had reached $1,000, one of the highest in the world and the highest in Latin America (IDB, 1975). In spite of this statistic, 73.7 percent of families in Venezuela have monthly incomes under $232, an amount which fails to provide the basic necessities for families with many children (Solarte, 1976). Furthermore, inflation has continued unabated and in 1975 the cost of living rose 11.2 percent (IDB, 1975).

According to a survey carried out in 1970 (Banco Obrero, 1972), monthly family income in towns of more than 10,000 inhabitants was distributed as shown in Table 16.

Salaries in urban areas tend to be higher than in rural areas: 53.6 percent of urban families receive less than $232 per month,

TABLE 16

Monthly Family Income in Towns of Over 10,000 Inhabitants

Income	Percent of Urban Population
698	10.2
350–697	19.1
232–349	17.1
116–231	30.5
70–115	12.15
70	10.7

Source: Banco Obrero, 1972.

while the figure for rural and urban areas combined is 73.7 percent. Families in the wage category under $232 have an average of four children under 18 years of age who have not yet entered the work force (Universidad Central de Venezuela, 1970).

NUTRITION AND HEALTH

A study of the 1950–1975 time period indicates that the general mortality rate has decreased from 10.9 deaths per 1,000 inhabitants in 1950 to 6.2 in 1975. During the same period infant mortality decreased from 79.9 to 43.7, and the mortality of the one to four year age group decreased from 11.6 to 3.8 per 1,000 (Osio Sandoval and Medina Colina, 1977). This impressive decrease in mortality has been attributed to the establishment, over the past 40 years, of maternal-infant care centers as well as to the availability of antibiotics (Osio Sandoval and Medina Colina, 1977).

The nutritional situation of surviving children, although better than in other Latin American countries, still presents serious problems. The mortality rate from malnutrition among children under five years of age is 38 per 100,000 with the highest risk occurring during the first two years of life (FIPAN, 1974). A survey carried out between 1976 and 1977, by the Instituto Nacional de Nutricion (INN), on a sample of 83,822 preschoolers (zero to six years of age) who attended health centers throughout the country indicated that 48.6 percent of these children were affected to some degree by malnutrition. When distributed into groups according to the Gomez classification, 36.2 percent had first-degree malnutrition, 10.9 percent second-degree, and 1.5 percent third-degree malnutrition (Osio Sandoval and Medina Colina, 1977). A report by COLUDES (Committee for the Fight Against Malnutrition) in November of 1974 presented figures similar to the INN survey. It indicates that 55 percent of all children in Venezuela between one and six years of age are malnourished and that 60 percent of all children in rural areas and 50 percent of all hospitalized children suffer some form of malnutrition. It is difficult to determine whether the rate of malnutrition has decreased or whether the 6 percent difference in figures represents an error factor. The latter explanation seems likely since several other sources indicate that the nutritional status of the country has changed little in the past 30 years (Bengoa et al., 1976; Borges Ramos, 1977). The most prominent problems seem to be: (1) deficient calorie intake; (2) deficient intake of high quality protein by certain population groups; (3) nutritional anemias, especially those due to iron deficiency; and (4) endemic goiter, which occurs primarily in the Andean region.

EDUCATION

The development of education in Venezuela is probably superior to that in Colombia and Peru, but it still presents a grim picture. In 1977 the illiteracy rate in Venezuela was 22.9 percent of the total population (Fundacion Mendoza, 1976a). Fundacion Mendoza (1976a) reports that in 1972-73 nearly 10 percent of the total primary school population dropped out, 21.6 percent of primary school age children were not enrolled in any public or private school, and an estimated 75 percent of high school age adolescents failed to enroll in school.

According to the Fundacion Festival del Nino (1976a, 1977), only 27 percent of preschoolers (age three to six) receive any form of educational assistance. Until the National Education reform of 1975, preschool education was not included in the regular curriculum and was regarded as a luxury. Today, efforts are being made to provide education for all preschoolers, but the lack of adequate facilities and teachers, and the failure to recognize the importance of formal preschool education, continue to hamper progress.

YOUNG CHILD POLICY IN VENEZUELA

There is little evidence that Venezuelan policy makers showed much concern for the growth and development of the young child during the decade of 1960-1970. The Ministry of Health concerned itself with the infant up to one year of age and the Ministry of Education cared for children over seven; for all practical purposes the preschool child was ignored (Fundacion Mendoza, 1972). The only agency dedicated to this age group was the Consejo Venezolano del Nino (CVN-Venezuelan Child Council), which was formed as an autonomous institution to safeguard the legal rights of children and to solve problems of adaptation, food, housing, and related social problems. A limited budget and scarce human resources, however, prevented it from achieving adequate coverage of preschoolers, the population segment in most need of its services.

Early efforts by the public sector to aid preschoolers tended to be illustrative and experimental, rather than resulting in the development of intervention programs. The Fundacion Festival del Nino was organized in 1964, but it was not until 10 years later that it established a definite policy. Now, utilizing the help of local mothers, it provides complete child care to children in marginal areas. The Federacion de Instituciones Privadas de Asistencia al Nino (Federation of Private Institutions to Help the Child—FIPAN) was organized in the early 1960s to unite 35 small private institutions whose separate efforts to help children achieved little. It now provides legal aid; coordinates and promotes the training and continuing education of professionals, technicians, and administrators in this field; and undertakes investigations into child-related issues.

In 1966 the Fundacion Mendoza, one of the agencies that operated under the aegis of FIPAN, organized a seminar to study the needs of the child. The participants concluded that: (1) insufficient aid was available for this population segment, (2) the lack of institutional coordination led to the duplication of existing efforts; and (3) no underlying policy united the variety of programs and projects in operation (Fundacion Mendoza, 1966). Participants in a second seminar, organized in 1977 to analyze the progress made during the previous decade, acknowledged the achievement of some progress but underscored the weaknesses of underlying program policy. Specific proposals were made for programs relating to: (1) development of parental responsibility; (2) increasing public awareness of the importance of the first 3 years of life; (3) provision of professional training in the field of child care; (4) creation of experimental units for testing new ideas in the child development field; (5) program participation by interested community members in order to compensate for the lack of available personnel; and (6) training grammar school children to care for their younger siblings (Fundacion Mendoza, 1977).

In 1976 three basic educational propositions were advanced by the government: (1) education is necessary for democracy; (2) education should be provided for everyone, taking into account individual needs; (3) education is necessary for the autonomous development of the country. These three policies imply a coverage of 500,000 preschoolers by 1980 (Fundacion Mendoza, 1977). At this same time, an increasing awareness of the nutrition problems became apparent. Carlos Andres Perez, the President of Venezuela, stated that:

> Our first problem, like that of all Latin America, is not, as is most commonly believed, the problem of education. It is, in fact, nutrition. Our rapid population growth has produced a situation in which at least 50 percent of our children suffer from malnutrition.

In this context a number of nutritional policies have been formulated within the last three years. Briefly, their aims may be summarized as follows:

1. The state guarantees the supply of essential nutritional products to the people in such a way that they will be available to those who need them.
2. Established mother-child health services are to be amplified so that effective nutritional protection is provided for the low-income sector of the population, particularly pregnant women, infants, preschoolers, the unemployed, and the worker. Basic nutrition education is to be transmitted via mass media.
3. Food will be produced in relation to the nutritional needs of the population, but will be imported until national production meets the levels of demand.
4. Transportation, storage, and distribution systems for food will be improved.
5. The quality of foods will be controlled.
6. Additional personnel will be trained in the field of food and nutrition (Osio Sandoval et al., 1976).

Whether or not these broad policies result in effective action is a question that requires careful analysis. While the formulation of policy indicates that the government is now focusing on social illnesses that affect young children, it is likely that some of the resulting programs may be launched without adequate coordination or underlying policy support.

THE CARACAS SETTING

Caracas, the most heavily populated city in Venezuela, is located in the north central region of the country. It is situated at 3,000 feet above sea level in a valley surrounded by the ranges of the central highlands. The last census (1971) measured the population at 2,183,935 or 20.3 percent of the national total. There are 964 inhabitants per square kilometer. Fifty-six percent of the city's population is under 20 years of age, only 4 percent is over 60, and the 43,902 preschoolers (0 to 6 years of age) in the Distrito Federal represent 19.8 percent of the population of this area (MSAS, 1976b). The growth rate in Caracas is 6 percent annually (Chen, 1970) and, if the rate is maintained, the population will reach 13 million by the year 2000. This prospect is unlikely, however, because of the limited resources of the area (Aguilera, 1975).

Child abandonment, which constitutes a serious problem in Caracas, may be viewed as symptomatic of the living conditions of the urban poor. One of the first efforts to determine the magnitude of the condition was made in 1944 when a survey was conducted by the CVN in the Distrito Federal and the states of Zulia, Sucre, Tachira, and Carababo. These areas were selected for study because of their extensive population and the variability of regional characteristics. Results of this survey indicated that 5.4 percent of the population between the ages of 0 and 18 years of age were abandoned; 16 percent were between 0 and 3 years and 28 percent were between 3 and 7 years. Both sexes were affected almost equally: 54 percent of the total were males and 46 percent were females. Study indicates that economic problems were the causal ingredients in most cases of abandonment (Solarte, 1976).

Another study, conducted by the CVN in 1973, involved 2,703 homes and 899 subjects from 0-18 years of age in metropolitan Venezuela; 2,062 homes and 5,796 subjects from the center of the city; and 641 homes and 3,203 subjects from marginal areas. The results indicated that the degree of abandonment for the studied population was 29.65 percent; 14.98 percent in the city center and 56.46 percent in the barrios. Twenty-four percent of the city center cases and 59.05 percent of those in the barrios were found among families with annual incomes below Bolivares (Bs.) 1,500 ($348.84); 44 percent of the families from both groups existed on diets which did not meet the required daily allowance; and 11 percent of the city center minors and 26 percent of those in the barrios were not attending school.

Daza (1977) reported on a socioeconomic survey conducted among 500 preschoolers attending day care programs in a marginal area of the city. The data showed that 70 percent of the children came from families with annual incomes under Bs. 1,000 ($232.56).

Only 7 percent were judged somatically healthy, while 22 percent were found to be anemic, 28.8 percent to have respiratory diseases, and 57.8 percent to be intellectually "below average." The study was presented in June 1977 at a national preschool seminar as "a sample of the true reality of what is happening to the health of the child that grows in the marginal areas." While the study is one of the few attempts to determine the state of health of preschoolers in Caracas, the report on the study does not include a description of either sample selection or data collection. A nutrition study carried out by the Instituto Nacional de Nutricion in 1976 on 6,222 preschoolers of the Sucre (part of metropolitan Caracas) showed that 63.6 percent were malnourished. The data breakdown is presented in Table 17. The prevalence figure for malnutrition (63.6 percent for a combination of first-, second-, and third-degree) is the highest among nine state surveys carried out during the same period (Osio Sandoval and Medina Colina, 1977). The results are particularly striking in view of the fact that Caracas has the highest number of preschool nutrition intervention programs in the country.

It should be noted, however, that the results of the studies just described may be taken only as partial indicators of the current situation. Their limited samples, possible selection bias, and the lack of reported data on the validity of procedures make it impossible to draw conclusive inferences from the results.

The importance of preschool interventions, with the emphasis on education, was realized by official agencies approximately 15

TABLE 17

Nutritional State of Preschool Children in Caracas

Nutritional State	Number	Percentage
Normal	2,268	36.4
First-degree malnutrition	8,867	46.1
Second-degree malnutrition	929	15.0
Third-degree malnutrition	158	2.5
	12,222	100.0

Source: INN.

years ago. Since then it has been necessary to train teachers, build facilities, establish programs, and explain to parents the importance of preschool education. Despite policy decisions and program implementation, the education of the preschooler in Caracas is still limited. As of October 1976 there were 67,799 children attending preschools in the Distrito Federal. This represents only 15.73 percent of the total preschool population of the area (Ministerio de Educacion, 1977). The next section will point out some of the many factors which account for this limited coverage.

INTERVENTION PROGRAMS

Most efforts concerning early intervention programs for preschoolers are mounted by individual organizations and, as a result, they operate without overall coordination. The following is a review of those activities of the Fundacion Festival del Nino, Consejo Venezolano del Nino, the Ministry of Education, and FIPAN that specifically emphasize either the prevention of mental retardation or the enhancement of cognitive development and preparation for formal primary schooling.

Fundacion Festival del Nino

This public organization, also called "Fundacion del Nino," has been in existence since 1964. Through the "Hogares de Cuidado Diario" and the "Centros Pre-escolares," it provides health, education, nutrition, and legal assistance to children 0 to 6 years of age. Approximately 7,170 children are presently serviced by this agency (Fundacion Mendoza, 1976a). In 1974, an institutional policy was first articulated and permanent programs were organized. The policy was divided into legal, social, and educational goals.

Legal: The organization attempts to assist those in low-income neighborhoods where programs of the Foundation have been established, by informing them of their rights and duties in connection with their children. The legal function also assists children who participate in the programs by ensuring that food and protection will be provided by their parents or representatives of the Foundation (Fundacion Festival del Nino, 1976d).

Social: Social activities are organized to help in the development of the neighborhood and the establishment of more relaxed and active communications among the people. The social coordination is carried out by one sociologist, two promotores (one of whom must be a sociologist and the other a social worker with a university degree),

and one coordinator of growth and development (who must also be a
university graduate) (Fundacion Festival del Nino, 1976e).

Educational: Preschoolers (0 to 6 years of age) are prepared
for primary school attendance by stimulation in areas of perception,
motor activities, cognitive development, and language. They participate in specific diagnostic activities which permit early recognition
of developmental problems or physical handicaps. Young volunteers
from the barrio are recruited to participate in the program (Fundacion
Festival del Nino, 1976b). At this point, the two programs of greatest
importance to the educational policy are the Hogares de Cuidado
Diario and the Preschool Centers.

Hogares de Cuidado Diario (home day care): These centers
are organized throughout the city to ensure that children of working
mothers receive medical supervision, a balanced diet, and mental
stimulation while their mothers are away. Participating children are
usually between the ages of 0 and 3, but sometimes older children
are accepted. The children attend from 7:00 A.M. to 5:00 P.M.,
Monday through Friday. In 1976 there were approximately 1,200
"Hogares" distributed among 52 barrios in Caracas; a total of 2,000
was projected for the end of 1977. The Foundation has divided the
city into sections of 20,000 inhabitants, each of which eventually will
have between 40 and 50 "Hogares."

A mother with one or two preschool children of her own is
selected from the community to care for up to six children of working
mothers from the same community. She is paid a salary and is given
additional funds to buy food for her charges. Selected women must:
(1) be able to read and write; (2) have proper sanitation facilities in
their homes; (3) be in good health; (4) have no more than two children
of their own under five years of age; and (5) be between the ages of
18 and 50 (Fundacion Festival del Nino, 1976c). Girls from the community who are 14 years or older and who have completed at least the
fifth year of primary school may assist in the care of the children.

More importantly, a team consisting of a social worker, a
teacher, and a "puerculturist" (a person trained in specific aspects
of child care—proper bathing, feeding, handling, and so forth) are
assigned to 20 "Hogares" in one barrio. The team is responsible for
the opening, maintenance, and supervision of each "Hogar." They
instruct caretaker mothers in the correct methods for stimulating
the children, teach the mothers how to prepare the menus provided
by the Instituto Nacional de Nutricion, and offer solutions to practical
problems encountered in the operation of the program. Monthly
meetings are held with caretaker mothers to clarify any additional
problems that arise. This appears to be the only training available
for caretaker mothers; they receive no special training before entering
the program. The teams of social workers, teachers, and puerculturists

are in turn supervised by a zone coordinator, a legal advisor, and a handicraft specialist who are responsible for 7 barrios (7 barrios equal 1 zone).

The "Hogar" arrangement is practical in that it uses people from the community as well as paraprofessionals to supplement the insufficient number of trained personnel. It has the added advantage of allowing the child to remain in his own environment; he is not obliged to travel long distances nor must he adapt to an environment with higher standards, such as a day care center. The "Hogares" program improves the environment of the child not by confronting him with strong environmental contrasts, but by gradually causing his own environment to change for the better. On the other hand, it is unreasonable to expect that caretaker mothers, with their lack of training, will be anything more than good baby sitters. Dr. H. J. Daza has prepared a rather critical report on the nutritional and health status of 500 children who were attending "Hogares" throughout the city (Daza, 1977). Unfortunately, he did not specify the length of time the children had been involved in the program before the study was made. He reports that: (1) 80 percent of the sample were found to be in a normal nutritional state, 14.40 percent showed mild malnutrition, 4.20 percent showed moderate malnutrition, and 1.40 percent were overweight; (2) 22 percent had anemia with a hematocrit level below 36; and (3) only 7 percent were found to be physically healthy.

If the children in this sample had been in the program for a period of time sufficient to allow them to improve their nutrition and health status, then these results seem to indicate that the program does not meet their needs. No other evaluation of program effectiveness has been made to date, however, so it is premature to judge whether or not the program is achieving its goals.

The Preschool Centers work as an alternative project to the "Hogares"; in general, however, children three years old or older attend the former type of institution. If funding restrictions or community size make it impossible to implement both programs in a given area, then the existing program must be adapted to fit the needs of the broader age group.

The Preschool Centers provide services from 8 to 12 hours per day in order to allow mothers to be permanently employed. Children receive breakfast, lunch, and a snack prepared according to the menus of the Instituto Nacional de Nutricion as well as a glass of milk and a soya cookie, both supplements from the INN. The program includes health evaluation for the children and advice and orientation for mothers on how to maintain good sanitary conditions and plan a balanced diet. The program includes direct and indirect teaching. The former consists of the traditional approach in which the adult explains an idea, concept, or activity to an individual child or to a group of children. Indirect teaching focuses on the child's active exploration and manipulation of materials offered by the center. This latter form follows a system of "Aula Abierta" developed by the Ministry of Education (see following section on Ministry of Education). The principal areas covered by this method are: motor and emotional development, social development, art, corporal expression, and science. A mimeographed guide for each of these areas has been written to serve as an aid for the teacher (Fundacion Festival del Nino, 1976a).

The "Aula Abierta" system is still in the experimental stage. No evaluation of the program as a whole has been attempted yet, but as each new technique is tested an evaluation is made of its effect and acceptance. Training of personnel involves one day of theory, in which the system is explained, and 15 days of on-site observations at an existing Preschool Center, for a total of 128 hours (Fundacion Festival del Nino, 1976a).

A family program in the education of children is offered at the center to assist parents to raise their social, cultural, and economic levels. The program consists of a series of "chats" on various aspects of child care, and parents are also encouraged to assist when parties or field trips are arranged for the children (Fundacion Festival del Nino, 1976a). Officials of the program indicate that, although it has been difficult to persuade parents to cooperate, their efforts are beginning to show beneficial results.

Evaluations of the children's social, verbal, and motor development are made at the time of enrollment in the program and are repeated a year later. Presently, however, these evaluations are superficial and not amenable to the collection of objective data. It is unlikely that they could be used to detect developmental changes.

Each center must have no less than 1.20 square meters of interior space per child and must care for at least 90 but not more than 150 children. Each adult must care for eight to ten children, if they are between 0 and 3 years of age, or for 15 to 17 children if they are between 3 and 6 years old (Fundacion Mendoza, 1976a).

Each center must have the following personnel per eight to 13 children:

1 director	1 coordinator	1 social worker
1 teacher	1 cook	2 psychologists
1 auxiliary	1 babysitter	1 auxiliary cook

There are now nine centers in Caracas caring for a total of 1,170 children between the ages of six months and six years (Fundacion Mendoza, 1976a).

TABLE 18

Distribution of Average Monthly Cost of Preschool Center

Personnel	Bs. 5,210.00	($1,211.63)
For 120 children	4,200.00	($976.75)
For 98 children	3,100.00	($720.93)
For 150 children	5,300.00	($1,232.56)
Utilities and materials	3,200.00	($744.19)
Other expenses (not explained)	8,546.00	($1,987.44)
Average monthly cost per child	176.30	($41.00)

Source: Fundacion Festival del Nino, 1976a.

The Preschool Center program is considerably more expensive than the "Hogares." More personnel are involved, and additional building facilities and more complex teaching materials are used. The average monthly cost per center is Bs. 21,156 ($4,920) (exchange rate: $1 = Bs. 430), distributed as shown in Table 18.

In summary, these are the existing intervention programs sponsored by the Festival del Nino. They are all relatively new programs and have undergone little or no evaluation. Thus it is still premature to determine whether or not they will be successful and, consequently, whether or not they will be expanded to other areas of the country.

Consejo Venezolano del Nino (CVN)

The CVN, founded on August 6, 1936, was one of the first public institutions in Venezuela concerned with the well-being of the child. Originally it was a part of the Ministry of Health and Social Assistance, but today it is part of the Ministry of Youth. It is funded by the General Budget of Rents and Public Expenses, but also receives donations from public and private sources.

According to a statement from the CVN, its objectives are: "To protect children between 0 and 6 years of age—children of working

mothers of low socioeconomic resources who work outside the home—
in order that they may have an adequate sociobiological development;
to direct social action towards the homes of the children attending
the program; and to offer family orientation to pregnant women"
(CVN, 1977).

The intervention programs sponsored by the CVN to help
preschoolers are the "Casa Cunas" for children 0 to 3 years of age
and the "Jardines de Infancia" for children four to six years old.
These two usually function as a unit offering nutrition, education,
and health assistance to the children.

The Jardine de Infancia program is similar in many ways to
the Preschool Center units of the Fundacion Festival del Nino: there
is some overlap between the two in terms of age groups covered, the
centers are spread throughout the city, preference is given to working
mothers, and the same kind of attention (health, nutrition, and education) is given to the children five days a week so that the mothers
may hold steady jobs. The program is based entirely on donations,
and works under the guidance of the Maternity Concepcion Palacios
and the Clinical Hospital of the Central University of Venezuela.

The CVN has decided to direct its attention towards children
from 3 to 6 years of age, and the "Casa Cunas" program for younger
children has been almost totally eliminated. This decision was made
in 1967, when there were 32 Casa Cunas throughout the city; in 1974
only five remained. The money and energy originally directed towards
the "Casa Cunas" is now being invested in the "Jardines de Infancia"
(Solarte, 1976). No explanation could be obtained for this change.

A pediatrician-puericulturist examines both child and mother
at the time of enrollment, and periodic weekly control checkups are
provided. A physician is also on call for any emergencies, and
odontologic care is offered at the odonto-pediatric center of the CVN.
The nutritional care consists of breakfast, lunch, and morning and
afternoon snacks as well as instructions for the children about which
foods are nutritious and how often they should be eaten. The menus
used are established by the INN (CVN, 1977).

Since 1975 education of the preschoolers has been based on
the system of "Aula Abierta" developed by the Ministry of Education.
(See following section on the Ministry of Education for details of this
program.) In essence the aim is to prepare the children for primary
schooling. Activities such as conversation, stories, music, folklore,
rhythm, puppet shows, games, excursions, and cultural events are
done by all the children together rather than individually or in smaller
groups as required by the new system (CVN, 1977). The Jardines
de Infancia also have a "Mothers Club" which attempts to orient the
mothers toward child care issues, and requests their cooperation in
the work done with the children (Solarte, 1976).

The teachers evaluate the development and progress of the children through direct observation. In addition, a battery of psychological tests, including the Stanford-Binet Intelligence Scale, is administered to the children. To date no published results are available on these evaluations.

Each Jardin de Infancia has the following personnel:

1 director, who must be a grammar school teacher and have at least
    three years experience with preschoolers
1 teacher (per 30 students) who must be a grammar school teacher
1 pediatrician-puericulturist
1 psychologist
1 music teacher
1 rhythm and folklore teacher
1 social worker and auxiliaries
1 economist
1 babysitter per teacher (CVN, 1977).

The estimated cost per child in a Jardin de Infancia is Bs. 2,303 ($535) annually and Bs. 191.90 ($44) monthly. In Caracas there are presently ten "Jardines de Infancia" attended by a total of 1,220 children; the two "Casa Cunas" that still remain care for 110 children. This implies a coverage of approximately 0.3 percent of the total preschool population of the city.

The CVN also seeks to find foster homes for abandoned children and, in cases of limited financial resources, may provide financial support for the chosen foster parents. In certain cases a couple is paid to care for and educate 30 children, but because of its high cost this home day care approach is not widespread (Solarte, 1976). The figures for the adoption program are extremely low. At present, of the 347 children placed in foster homes throughout Venezuela, most are in Caracas. The officials in charge of matters of adoption also handle legal problems related to the moral, medical, and economic well-being of children (CVN, 1973).

Ministry of Education

Although the Ministry of Education has existed for over 100 years, its interest in preschool education began in 1966. A study made at that time, to determine the quality and coverage of 64 day care centers in Caracas, revealed that teachers lacked instructional materials and that as a result their activities were aimless (OMEP, 1974). Accordingly, the first official preschool program was created and tested in seven day care centers. Changes and adaptations were made until 1969 when the program was officially accepted (OMEP, 1974). Since then annual courses have been conducted to train teachers in the use of this program (Fundacion Mendoza, 1977).

In 1970 the Department of Preschool Education was formed within the Ministry of Education. Its functions were:

1. To advise the Ministry of the policies, objectives, and aims necessary to help the preschooler.

2. To coordinate the execution of the strategies established in the "Plan de La Nacion" (national plan of action established every five years with the change of president) for the development of preschool education.

3. To organize, direct, coordinate, supervise, and control the units and services established for this cause.

4. To promote the incorporation of the family, official and private institutions, and the community in general for the benefit of preschool education (Fundacion Mendoza, 1977).

With the opening of a special department for preschoolers, national enrollment rose from 30,863 preschoolers in 1966-1967 to 224,000 in 1975-76. The goal is to incorporate 300,000 children by 1979: its achievement will require a total of 12,500 day care centers, 12,500 teachers, and 12,500 auxiliaries (OMEP, 1974).

One of the serious problems faced by the Ministry in achieving its goal is the availability of space. A 1977 survey indicated that in the entire country only 3,402 classrooms were used for preschool education. Of these, 2,182 had been especially built, 747 were remodeled rooms, and 473 were unadapted grammar school rooms or rooms in large houses which were not adequate for a preschool center. According to the "V Plan de La Nacion," 2,793 new classrooms are to be built yearly. Even if this goal is met, and 8,989 classrooms are available by 1979, a shortage of 4,511 rooms will exist from the number necessary to incorporate 300,000 children into the preschool educational system (Vasquez Marquez, 1975).

The shortage of teachers with heterogeneous training is another obstacle. Eighty-five percent of the teachers have no training in preschool education; most are primary school teachers transferred by the Ministry to the new department. Of the remaining 15 percent, some have taken intensive courses to update their training and a small number have received adequate training. In 1974-1975, there was a total of 5,030 teachers throughout the country. This represents a ratio of 1 teacher to 369 students registered in public preschools (Vasquez Marquez, 1975).

In the Distrito Federal in 1976 there were 417,138 preschoolers from 0 to 6 years of age (MSAS, 1976b); of these, only 26,283 were cared for in public facilities. This figure represents only 6.3 percent of the total population of this age group (Ministry of Education, 1976). No precise information could be obtained on the number of teachers in the Distrito Federal or in metropolitan Caracas.

The existing official preschool program is based on the primary school program. The subjects covered are basically the same (Vasquez Marquez, 1975). There has been much discussion about this program, and officials of the Ministry now generally agree that preschoolers have different needs than older children and should, therefore, have a special program which takes these needs into account. In view of this, the present program is in the process of being revised.

The current edition has been in use since 1974. It covers six basic areas, each with a defined number of activities (Ministerio de Educacion, 1974):

Area	Number of Activities
Language and Literature	23
Science and Mathematics	49
Social Studies	37
Plastic Arts	40
Education for the Home	8
Physical Education	10
Music	17

One of the most important projects of the Ministry of Education is the "Aula Abierta" educational system now being implemented in a number of preschools throughout Caracas. This system presents a methodology for classroom instruction of young children. The class area is divided into seven sections, each containing games and materials peculiar to one area of development: art, construction, carpentry, drama, science, quiet games, and cooking. The children select the sections they wish to attend each day. Work groups are made up of six or seven children, but each child works at his own level; teachers only intervene to guide children and assist them when they request help. Music and physical education activities are carried out by the group as a whole.

The theory behind this method of teaching is (1) that preschool children have different rhythms and styles of learning, (2) that they learn through experience, (3) that learning is more effective when they plan their own activities, and (4) that they learn as much from other children as from the teacher. These principles are a significant departure from the directed teaching approach. A preliminary evaluation report shows that children exposed to this system have shown greater interest in their subjects, more independence, and more self-assurance than students educated in the traditional method (Loreto de Perez, Chavez de Romero, and Fermin, 1976).

MEVAL, another experimental project, has been organized and financed by the Ministry of Education and the Van Leer Foundation. The program operates in three marginal areas in Caracas and each center offers nutrition, recreation, education, and clothing (Fundacion Mendoza, 1976a). The program began in 1974 with the opening of one unit in the barrio "Santa Ana de Carapita." Two other units were opened on the basis of experience gained from the original operation; one in the "23 de Enero" and the other on the road to "La Guaira." Their general objective is to establish an alternative system of preschool care which will compensate for the scarcity of facilities and teachers. At the same time, the project hopes to awaken the community to the importance of preschool care (Fundacion Mendoza, 1976a).

MEVAL is somewhat similar to the Preschool Centers of the Fundacion Festival del Nino and the Jardines de Infancia of the CVN. In the MEVAL project, however, personnel directly in contact with the children are people from the barrio who have been specially trained. Also, an underlying interest of MEVAL investigation is to find the most efficient way to extend the program throughout the country at minimum cost. The other institutions described are more interested in relieving the present situation than in addressing future problems.

Approximately 1,030 children are presently being cared for in three centers. In addition, three mobile units rotate among the centers; one medical, one odontologic, and one pedagogic (supplies audio-visual aids and other equipment). Five more centers are under construction (Fundacion Mendoza, 1976a).

The teachers in this program are community members who live in the area where the center is located. The only requirement for selection is that they be able to read and write and that they have a good disposition. Those selected are given 130 hours of specialized instruction and three weeks of teacher training before they are allowed to proceed on their own. Each teacher cares for 30 children and generally works part-time. Male teachers instruct the children in growing vegetables, raising animals, and caring for other children when they are in the park areas (Fundacion Mendoza, 1976a).

There are two coordinators per center and, at the beginning of the program, each completes a course covering infant behavior, evolutionary psychology, preschool teaching, and elements of psychology, and participates in a workshop on expression. In addition, each coordinator completes 30 hours of practical work. This training is given to equalize and evaluate the capacity of the personnel.

Although no evaluation of this program has been made, officials informed the investigator that they were pleased with the results that they had observed to date. They noted that the attitude of the barrio population had changed a great deal since the program was initiated, and that community members showed more interest in the program, a greater willingness to cooperate, and that, in general, they were more friendly to the children.

Federacion de Instituciones Privadas
de Asistencia al Nino (FIPAN)

FIPAN, a private, nonprofit organization founded in 1958, groups together 32 private institutions that provide services for children, adolescents, and families (FIPAN, 1975a). Its role is to strengthen and develop the institutions it represents by means of promotion, stimulus, and coordination of their various activities. Member organizations cooperate in the general objective of enhancing the development of children and thereby helping in the process of the country's development (FIPAN, 1975a).

FIPAN's activities may be described as follows:

1. To advise member institutions on matters relating to specific activities and to help them establish priorities of action.

2. To coordinate their work so that each institution is able to offer technical assistance to the others whenever possible.

3. To represent these institutions in legal matters.

4. To promote the coordination of their activities with those of the public sector: the Ministry of Health, the Ministry of Education, and so forth.

5. To offer courses designed to improve the competency of the personnel in participating institutions.

6. To investigate problems which affect the growth and development of children.

FIPAN does not plan the programs of member institutions; each one maintains its identity, sets up its own programs, and arranges its own financing. FIPAN offers advice and aid only when it is requested by member institutions. The federation is maintained by a yearly quota of Bs. 1,000 ($232.59) per institution, by a few private donations, and by charges levied for selected services (FIPAN, 1975a). The investigator was informed that in 1975 a total of 4,995 preschoolers attended day care centers within FIPAN. One hundred forty other children received care in "Casa Cunas." The following is a description of member institutions which provide services to preschool children.

Most of the participating institutions have small scale operations. The YMCA, one of the organizations visited, has been affiliated with FIPAN since 1958. It has run a small day care center since 1973 in Catia, an old, low-income section of the city, which cares for the preschoolers of working mothers in the area. They care for children from four to six years of age, five days a week in two sessions, one in the morning and one in the afternoon.

The morning session has 38 children and is directed by one teacher who is paid by the YMCA. She plans her own program, alternating a half-hour of guided activity with a half-hour of free play. The afternoon session has 35 children, is led by a teacher sent by the Ministry of Education, and follows the program established by the Ministry (see previous section on Ministry of Education). Both teachers work under the supervision of a director who is also in charge of the maintenance of the center; this is the extent of the personnel involved. Children bring their own food, and no medical services are available. Each child pays Bs. 15 ($.50) per month to cover the morning teacher's salary and cost of the materials used in class.

Most of the other preschool care institutions in FIPAN have an organization similar to this one. Four are Catholic associations and four others are run by women's associations. The emphasis is on custodial care or preparation for formal schooling. Two centers belonging to these institutions, the "Centro Don Bosco" which belongs to the Asociacion Femenina de Educacion Social (Feminine Association for Social Education) and the "Virgin Nina" of the Juventud Catolica Femenina Venezolana (Venezuelan Feminine Catholic Youth) have been used by FIPAN to try out its program of Family Education. This program, funded by UNICEF, includes a set of activities which will help the child to know himself, his relation to other members of his family, his sex, and his basic needs (FIPAN, 1976).

The first children to participate in this program were selected from urban families of low socioeconomic level. This population generally has a weak family structure, adaptation problems caused by migration from rural areas, and frustrated expectations (Fundacion Mendoza, 1972). The guide provided by FIPAN for use in these two

centers covers one topic each day. For example, a day may be devoted to the child's gradual recognition that the people the child lives
with form a family, or to the differences between a boy and a girl.
The teacher observes the interest that the children have in each of
these topics, gives explanations and answers questions, and will help
clarify their doubts (FIPAN, 1976).

The pilot program was very successful; at the end of the experimental period the preschoolers who participated in the program
showed greater awareness of the family structure, more communication with their parents and peers, and a clearer perception of the
roles of adults than did the children in the control groups (FIPAN,
1974).

The Fundacion Mendoza also operates a small-scale program
which, because of its duration and experimental quality, has probably
influenced the field of child care in Venezuela more than any other.
Its objective is to provide care and education for children of all
races, religions, and socioeconomic groups, although preference is
given to the children of working mothers. It maintains close contact
with the parents of the participating children, and elicits their cooperation with the child's education. This center also serves as an
observation and practice center for the preschool teachers who are
being prepared by the Universidad Metropolitana.

The Fundacion Mendoza began caring for children in November of 1951 when it opened the "Luisa Goiticoa" day care center.
The center is located in Moriperez, an area of rapid population
growth, and has the capacity to care for 150 children. The personnel of the center consists of a director, five specialized teachers,
six auxiliaries, and one each of the following: music teacher, pedi-
atrician, odontologist, psychologist, social worker, economist, and
nurse. The ratio of adults to children is 1 to 26 for the younger
group (3- and 4-year-olds) and 1 to 32 for the older children (5 and
6 years of age) (Fundacion Mendoza, 1976b). Breakfast, lunch, and
an afternoon snack are provided and children are under permanent
medical supervision. In cases where additional care is necessary,
they are sent to the Children's Hospital.

The monthly cost per child is Bs. 310 ($72.09) and is divided
as shown in Table 19. Charges are based on ability to pay. In 1976
56.19 percent of the cost was covered by the Foundation and 43.81
percent by the parents.

Since February of 1975, the center has been following the
"Aula Abierta" educational system, patterned after the experimental
steps of the Ministry of Education (see previous section on Ministry
of Education). This change from the traditional arrangement required a reorientation of the teachers and teaching aids. As the
students and teachers have adapted to the new system, they have

TABLE 19

Distribution of Monthly Cost of Day Care Center

	Percentage
Director and teachers	36.68
Medical and social	10.83
General services	15.83
Food	17.92
Other expenses	12.08
Depreciation	6.67

Source: Fundacion Mendoza, 1976b.

acknowledged the existence of beneficial changes. The children have shown behavioral independence, capacity to relate to others, control of impulses, and autonomy. Completion of a formal evaluation was scheduled for June 1978 (Duran de Vargas, 1977).

It is apparent from an interview with the officials of this operation that they maintain no contact with other day care centers. They are not aware of the number of centers which operate in the city, nor of the programs they follow. Lack of information and communication is a general problem in Caracas, but it is particularly distressing in this case, not only because it involves the oldest, most renowned, and best organized center, but also because the center was experimenting with the "Aula Abierta" system which is used by several other centers.

FIPAN has worked hard to maintain open communication between various private and public institutions working for the welfare of children. Unfortunately, most of the institutions it represents are small, and, as a result, their actions have limited influence on the problems which affect the preschooler in Caracas.

CONCLUSIONS

At present there are a number of agencies in Caracas (four of which were reviewed in this chapter) working on behalf of the preschooler of low socioeconomic level. Some of the agencies offer complete care (that is, nutrition, health, and education), while others focus on only one aspect of development. Together these institutions cover approximately 20 percent of the total preschool population of the city (Eskenasy, 1978).

At the present time there is considerable duplication of work among agencies, and no attempt is being made to coordinate activities. As noted in the previous section, the Fundacion Festival del Nino, the Consejo Venezolano del Nino, MEVAL, and several of the private organizations of FIPAN are all offering similar programs of complete day care; that is, the same nutritional, educational, and health aspects are handled by each agency individually. Each agency has its own administrators, coordinators, and supervisors as well as personnel who are in direct contact with the children. It is evident that a need exists for an agency to coordinate all the activities, at least those occurring in the public sector. Improving coordination and communication among agencies would increase the proportion of the preschool population served.

It has been apparent also in this review that many of the evaluation methods used by the institutions are deficient. This state of affairs leads to heterogeneity in the results obtained and to an increasing tendency to deliberately refrain from providing a clear picture of a given situation. Another major shortcoming of the observed programs was their geographical location; they were seldom close to the populations with the greatest need. As in the cases of Peru and Colombia, previously described, the result is isolation of the most deprived groups.

9
CONCLUSIONS

This chapter presents specific conclusions based on the pre-ceding review of child development and early intervention programs in Latin America. Although there are grounds for claiming objec-tivity and comprehensiveness in the preparation of these conclusions, the reader should be aware that what follows is determined by the author's interests, biases, and judgment of relevance. Moreover, the conclusions are restricted by the limits of the data presented.

The conclusions are designed to be read, interpreted, and used without the necessity of referring to preceding chapters. The question and answer format, a style of proven effectiveness (Lappe and Collins, 1977), will aid those readers who are not interested in the specifics of program implementation or research undertaking, but who wish to get to the heart of the monograph. The questions presented are those likely to be posed by policy-makers concerned with issues of child development in Latin America.

Three major subject areas will be covered: the nature of intellectual derangements associated with poverty and malnutrition; program modalities and effectiveness; and unresolved issues. In keeping with the spirit of this monograph, all answers are based primarily on Latin American studies.

NATURE OF INTELLECTUAL DERANGEMENTS
ASSOCIATED WITH POVERTY AND MALNUTRITION

Question: How valid is the often-repeated statement that poverty and malnutrition have adverse effects on the development of intelligence?

Answer: If intelligence is defined in terms of either IQ scores from intelligence or developmental scale measures, or educational success, then studies in Latin America present solid, consistent evidence of the adverse effects of poverty and malnutrition. In comparison to middle- or high-income children, low-income children achieve lower scores on intelligence tests (IQ and DQ), perform less well in academic settings, and are more likely to drop out of school. Test performance will be even poorer among low-income children who are also undernourished. Among populations where malnutrition is endemic, the prevalence of mental retardation is higher than in those populations where malnutrition is not a public health problem.

Question: It is said that intelligence tests do not measure cognitive behavior. If that is so, why should one worry about low IQ scores?

Answer: Most intelligence tests include a number of subtests which assess abilities such as vocabulary development, concept formation, or perceptual organization. These same abilities are developed in formal schooling and fit in with the demands of an industrial society. It is this continuity in the development of those mental skills which are rewarded by the social system that explains why test scores obtained at age seven may be relatively good predictors of later educational achievement. Functionally, therefore, it may not matter whether an IQ test, or a test of a specific cognitive ability, reflects innate abilities or not; to the extent that it is predictive of performance in school, or in an industrial setting, it provides useful information. This is particularly true if the concern is with incorporation of children into an industrial society. Conversely, if the concern is with the adjustment capabilities of the child relative to a particular social milieu, or ecology (such as a preindustrial setting), then it is unlikely that the intelligence test will be useful. For example, an IQ test may be inappropriate if the goal is to assess the psychological adaptation of a native child to a isolated rural area of the Andes.

Question: Is it not possible that, in essence, the socioeconomic structure of Latin America may be a function of innate differing abilities, or that intergenerational malnutrition and poverty have taken their toll?

Answer: The Latin American studies reviewed in this manuscript have demonstrated that the mental abilities of these children are not static. Indeed, there are clear indications that if a three-year-old child is enrolled in a program involving betterment of living conditions (for example, improvements in diet, health, and learning opportunities), major upward changes can occur in test performances relating to general cognitive ability. Moreover, analysis of the test performances of eight-year-old children living in impoverished environments indicate that these children possess abilities which reflect strong but undeveloped potential.

Question: In connection with the issue of age, is it possible to specify at what point the child is more vulnerable to the adverse effects of poverty and malnutrition?
Answer: From the data available on Latin America, it is almost impossible to give a conclusive answer to this question. Any valid answer must take into account the severity, duration, and interactions of these conditions, as well as the age factor. In connection with malnutrition specifically, if the condition is severe and of several months duration during the first year of life, there is a high probability that it will seriously jeopardize the development of intelligence. By contrast, if the condition is severe but acute (short duration) and occurs during the second year of life, the chances of full rehabilitation are high.

It is also apparent that the interaction of poverty and malnutrition increases the probability of cognitive deficiency among low-income children who are malnourished. It is not clear why this occurs, however, because the nature of the interactions among both sets of conditions remains unknown.

Question: Is the prevalence of malnutrition and poverty in Latin America of sufficient magnitude to be a public health concern?
Answer: The data reviewed on prevalence of malnutrition and extent of poverty have been limited to South America and restricted to a few regions of the Andean countries. Although some statistics are encouraging (for example, drop of childhood mortality in Venezuela), most of the information creates a dismal picture of the number of children living in poverty and the small chance they have to develop normally. Twenty years from now some of these countries may have over two million infants and preschoolers living in conditions of extreme poverty (for example, Colombia, Peru, Bolivia).

The cities of Bogota, Caracas, Lima, and Medellin, among others, have urban growth rates approaching 6 percent annually. The result is an accelerated creation of squatter settlements, or shanty towns, where the number of infants and preschool children may account for approximately 25 percent of the total population. In some nutrition surveys in such low-income, overcrowded areas, almost half of the children studied presented signs of malnutrition. In some Latin American regions, malnutrition has been associated with almost half of the cases of childhood mortality. Moreover, the GNP growth rate in most of the countries is not large enough to project that it will solve the problems of poverty and malnutrition in the near future.

Question: From what is known about the adverse effects of low socio-economic conditions and malnutrition on behavioral development, is it possible to specify which factors have the most serious effects, in order to establish priorities for planning programs?

Answer: First it should be noted that not all poor children are malnourished. The converse, however, is nearly always true. Second, poverty, both with and without malnutrition, may have adverse effects on cognition, but in terms of impact on the population the effects of poverty are more likely to be serious than are the effects of poverty and malnutrition combined. On the basis of numbers alone the issue of poverty should have priority over malnutrition.

In situations where socioeconomic factors and undernutrition coexist, a number of unsuccessful attempts have been made to establish the specific and separate effects of each on cognitive development. The effects appear to be intertwined so intimately that, given the levels of conceptualization, study design, and statistical techniques available, it may be impossible to parcel out one set of variables in order to estimate the effects of the others. It is conceivable, because of this tight interaction, that interventions restricted to dietary supplementation have not shown any strong beneficial effects over behavioral development.

Briefly, what is known is that (1) if priority is to be determined by the number of children likely to have an environmentally induced cognitive deficit, then the focus must be on poverty in general; (2) if priority is to be determined by severity of cognitive deficits, then the focus should be placed on the poor and undernourished, especially the severely undernourished; and (3) if priority is to be determined by concern for immediate action, then the focus must not be on food supplementation alone, but on a comprehensive approach linking nutrition, health, and psychoeducational stimulation.

Question: Most studies that explored effects of poverty and malnutrition on the psychological development of children focused on cognition. Are there any other effects, such as on motivational or socioemotional development?

Answer: Although these other psychological dimensions are extremely important elements of the developmental process, no systematic and well-controlled studies have focused on them. Thus, it is impossible at this point to make a conclusive statement concerning the nature, if any, of such effects. Anecdotal and clinical descriptions have pointed out that the malnourished child is apathetic, withdrawn, and lacks motivation. These descriptions are too general and vague to aid in understanding the scope and seriousness of the effects. More data are necessary before any conclusive inferences can be drawn.

PROGRAM MODALITIES AND EFFECTIVENESS

Question: What kinds of programs are currently being run in Latin America?

Answer: There appear to be broad trends in early intervention programs. The first is toward development of national programs under the auspices of governmental agencies (that is, Ministries of Education) and/or of a national child welfare agency (for example, Colombia, Chile, Peru). These national programs are generally center-based affairs, with a national curriculum, and the intent is to apply them throughout the country. Moreover, they tend to include, in addition to an educational component, dietary supplementation (for example, breakfast or lunch) and health surveillance. The second trend is toward development of pilot programs by semiprivate or private agencies, groups of concerned individuals, or even special sections of Ministries of Health or Education. In most cases there is both a service and research orientation, the latter primarily in the form of an evaluation. Programs are generally of short duration (2 years). In a few cases, the programs include nutrition supplementation; in all of them the axis of the intervention is an educational component, which is either directed to the child or to the mother. Examples of these programs are the Programa Piloto de Estimulacion Precoz in Chile and the Hogares de Cuidado Diario in Colombia. The third trend is toward quasi-experimental* programs and grew out of academic concerns for the specific effects of malnutrition on mental development. In these programs the research component is the primary undertaking. All of them have included nutrition supplementation and a few have included an educational component as well (for

---

*By quasi-experimental studies we mean investigations in given social settings where the investigator introduces an experimental variable (for example, food supplement) in order to assess its effects over a specified outcome variable (for example, somatic growth). However, the investigator lacks control over a number of variables which may confound the effects of the experimental over the outcome variable (Campbell and Stanley, 1973).

example, the longitudinal studies on nutrition and mental development at INCAP in Guatemala, or ICBF in Bogota, Colombia).

Question: Is there a unifying philosophy throughout these programs?
Answer: The working hypothesis of all programs is that poverty and malnutrition have adverse effects on the mental development of young children; program goals are to prevent or ameliorate those effects. All projects, except those in which intervention is restricted to nutrition supplementation, appear to operate under the assumption that parental behavior, or conditions intrinsic to families living in extreme poverty, fail to foster intellectual competence. Accordingly, they assume that the introduction of relevant modifications to old conditions and behavior, or the development of new conditions and behavior, will have salutary effects and foster cognitive growth. None of these programs have postulated any relationships between intrinsic family conditions and the social, political, and economic forces of society that create them.

Question: Are these programs effective?
Answer: The diversity of opinion on the nature of effectiveness is such that an answer to the question probably requires multiple qualifications. For example, effectiveness in terms of what developmental parameter? Within psychological development the focus has been restricted to cognitive growth. As previously indicated, little effort has been made to detect other developmental benefits derived from these interventions. Moreover, although a few studies have investigated effects on caretaking, this area has not been satisfactorily explored. It is not clear, for example, whether changes in maternal behavior are long-lasting or whether the beneficial effects of those changes extend beyond termination of the intervention.

A simple generalization concerning mental development, and one which encompasses the results of most of the programs reviewed, is that cognitive growth is a plastic process, one which responds to intervention. By the same token it must be inferred that this plasticity facilitates both gains and losses. None of the programs has demonstrated that beneficial effects on cognitive growth last for a significant length of time following termination of the intervention. It is possible, for example, that gains demonstrated during periods of intervention may be erased if formal schooling is inadequate or if the child continues to live in an economically impoverished environment.

It is also possible to make generalizations about treatment modes. Although most studies have not compared effectiveness of treatment methods, it appears that comprehensive interventions are the most successful. Comprehensive interventions are those programs which include not only dietary supplementation appropriate to meet physiological growth requirements, but also health surveillance and creation of learning environments. (An example is the integrated approach of the CAIPs in Colombia, see Chapter 6.) Monofocal interventions, such as those limited to food supplementation, have provided benefits which are nearly negligible in terms of cognitive growth. Some of these studies may have shown statistically significant correlations between supplementation level and performance level in cognitive tests, but these measures are numerically small and their biological significance has yet to be determined. Conversely, long-term (13 years) programs which include nutrition supplementation, health surveillance, and educational inputs have shown overt effects on mental development.

Although some generalizations may be valid, it is usually an error to lump all programs together in order to assess program effectiveness. Given the differences in the nature of the projects, assessments of success require criteria appropriate for each type of program. For example, in comparison to national programs, the quasi-experimental programs discussed were relatively small academic undertakings, but were built on research infrastructures with very large budgets (see Chapter 4). These programs were well equipped to supervise the mechanics of the operation (that is, attending to a feeding station, or pedagogical activities in a day care center), and the time and funds available allowed them to maintain strict standards in personnel selection. Given the enormity of the task, a national program (see Chapters 7 and 8) which runs on a limited budget, and is built on an established bureaucracy, is not able to maintain an optimal operation. In some situations the philosophy of the program may be totally distorted. In addition, great caution must be exercised in the generalization of results from a quasi-experimental project to a national program. A program that works in a limited situation may not duplicate its success in a large-scale operation.

Question: Because cost is an important consideration in program implementation, it is crucial to focus on those cases with the greatest developmental risk. Is it possible to define a target age for programs, and the length of time children should attend?

Answer: The data are neither clear enough nor comprehensive enough to give conclusive answers, but some inferences are warranted. It appears that up to about 18 months of life, short-term (~3 to 6 months) and long-term (~12 months) interventions result in similar cognitive gains. Moreover, comparisons of the developmental quotients of low- and high-income-level infants up to approximately 15 months show that while there may be some between-group differences in the expected direction, these differences are small. In contrast to these observations, however, the data on severe protein-energy malnutrition show that long-term malnutrition in the first year of life may result in serious cognitive derangements. Accordingly, the only conclusion warranted by the limited data is that unless the target population is at risk of severe biosocial deprivation, interventions may be delayed until after the first year of life.

On the other hand, data from well-controlled comprehensive interventions beginning at about 36 to 42 months and continuing for about 4 years (about 9 months per year) show meaningful gains in general cognitive ability at the termination of treatment. Moreover, these gains vary as a function of age at time of intervention and duration of treatment; the younger the child (within an approximate range of 36 to 80 months) at the beginning of the treatment, the greater the impact of the program. It should be noted, however, that, even following the largest gains, the level of performance of the children exposed to the treatment does not equal the level of performance of middle- or high-income children.

If maximum results are to be achieved from intervention strategies, it is necessary for the child to be initiated into the program between the ages one and three and to continue in the program as long as it is feasible—if possible up to the initiation of formal education.

Question: What age group receives the greatest emphasis in intervention programs? Do programs take into account the developmental differences among infants, toddlers, and preschoolers?

Answer: Most programs, especially those which are nationwide, emphasize the preschool age group. The quasi-experimental programs are the exception. No established policy attributes greater developmental importance to this age; indeed, many of those involved in such programs recognize the importance of the infancy and toddler periods and question the wisdom of restricting the focus primarily to the preschooler.

The emphasis on the preschooler seems to result from the interaction of two factors. First, it is relatively easy to work with preschoolers because they are able to communicate verbally and move around on their own. Programs for infants and toddlers, on the other hand, not only require a greater number of adults for caretaking and overall supervision, but additional physical care facilities (cribs, and so forth) as well. Second, there are well-established pedagogical concepts which serve as the bases for the preparation of materials or curricula for the preschooler. Conversely, in Latin America there is a scarcity of theoretical guidelines concerning the most beneficial psychoeducational approach to take in working with the infant and toddler. Even among those quasi-experimental programs which include a psychoeducational intervention directed at the early stages of development, operational definitions for their intervention are weak and lack coherence. Moreover, some of the better controlled studies have required reanalysis of the work done in order to define the nature of the intervention. In addition, the nature of the changes in mental development that occur during this period are not well understood, and the factors which foster competence and development are not yet well defined.

Question: Is there any intervention program of proven effectiveness which can be used as a prototype for Latin America?
Answer: To discuss a prototype would represent a naive disregard for the deep-rooted cultural, social, economic, and even physical-ecological differences that exist among the regions of Latin America. Even if the focus is placed on the Andean countries, and if common denominators are found among large cities such as Bogota, Caracas, Lima, and Santiago, existing differences must be taken into account in developing programs for children. Similarities in the rural-urban process in these cities may hide important differences among the migrants themselves in terms of patterns of family organization, nutritional status, dietary habits, and educational level of the parents. Such differences may be important enough to determine different levels of success in programs with face validity (for example, food supplementation). The indicators on social, cultural, and economic characteristics that should be taken into account in order to create an ad hoc program are, as yet, undetermined. Programs have been created without consideration of the idiosyncratic characteristics of the recipients even though these characteristics should mold the intervention strategy of the programs. In general, the success of established modes of operation is assumed.

Question: What factors have limited the effectiveness of these programs?
Answer: Given the differences in the nature of the programs, it is difficult to identify common factors which interfered with the effectiveness of all programs. Moreover, the nature of criteria for effectiveness may also vary between programs. In the case of the quasi-experimental studies, effectiveness must be measured in terms of their research goals, while among most of the community and national programs, effectiveness must be evaluated in the context of service delivery. Thus, this question demands selective responses rather than one general answer. Here the focus will be on the quasi-experimental studies and on the national programs.

The food delivery components of these studies have not been completely successful because of the lack of compliance on the part of potential recipients. In many cases the index subjects either did not use the free food or used it as a substitute for part of their regular diet rather than as a supplement. These differences in behavior contributed to intake variability which, instead of facilitating data interpretation, further confounded it. This problem occurs because of the well-known difficulty in obtaining low-error intake data in the household, and is particularly evident in those studies with weak research designs (that is, those with no control group).

In connection with psychoeducational inputs, it has been difficult to specify the precise nature of the intervention, particularly in the case of home visits made by research auxiliary personnel for the purpose of working with the mothers. In these cases clear operational descriptions of the stimulation process were absent, but it was assumed that all staff involved in this part of the study shared the same concepts, followed the same strategies, and had similar goals and expectations for their work. These assumptions, however, are not supported by data and it may be that significant variations did exist within what was nominally the same treatment.

The lack of assessments of possible treatment-context interactions in the quasi-experimental studies constitutes a related limitation. Accordingly, it is possible that the observed outcomes were not derived from the treatment itself, but from intervening variables activated by the treatment. For example, food supplementation may have alerted the mothers to attend to the different developmental needs of the child, and this more concentrated attention then may have fostered the overall development of the child.

To measure the effectiveness of national programs (that is, the program in Chile) it is necessary to assess the quantity and quality of service delivery. It is apparent from the review of programs in three Andean countries (Colombia, Peru, Venezuela), that while these programs may reach a relatively large number of children in terms of absolute numbers, comparatively speaking they are far from reaching a substantive number of the total population requiring these services. Moreover, the absentees generally are those children with greatest risk of developmental derangements—those who live in extreme poverty. These facts are particularly troublesome when projected into the future. In at least one case, expenditures already made suggest that further expansion at the present rate would be financially unwise because the nature of the benefits is yet to be determined.

The effectiveness of large-scale programs has also been jeopardized by poor administrative infrastructure, and lack of both staff training and competency. In the three countries studied, inadequate technical and administrative communication between central and regional or community centers, or between programs in Venezuela, often resulted in isolation of centers or programs. This situation in turn resulted in performance levels far below standards set for the operation. Unfortunately, such a situation often occurs in programs which address the needs of the most deprived groups of children; the product then becomes a total distortion of what was originally intended. Moreover, it is often these cases which, because of poor training and overall preparation, display the most serious problems in staff competency.

Question: What has been the community response to these programs?
Is there evidence of receptivity and cooperation?
Answer: Some of the projects reviewed provide clear evidence of community interest in the implementation, development, and goals of programs on behalf of young children. This interest may have been the result of free access to a specific good brought from the outside (that is, food) or the result of concern for the growth and development of young children (as in Puno, Peru). With one or two exceptions (Plaza Pre-escolar, Chile), however, no systematic data have been collected on community interest and response. Accordingly, it is presently impossible to analyze overall community response and determine how the implementation of a program could be facilitated or hindered by such responses.

It may be inferred from observations that interest in or response to a program will depend on the nature of the service offered and its face validity. Response to a home visitors program, for example, may well depend upon the range of useful information which the visitor can provide in connection with caretaking and other family affairs. Likewise, the face validity and immediate benefits of the program may modulate the community response. In one case, for example (food supplementation in Mexico, see Table 4), the impressive physical growth of the participants created a major interest in the study within the community.

UNRESOLVED ISSUES

The third group of questions and answers has been divided into two subgroups, according to the nature of the unresolved issues to which they are addressed. One subgroup refers to justification for further investments in preschool interventions, and the second focuses on ways of facilitating the implementation of new programs. All questions posed have been presented, either implicitly or explicitly, within the first eight chapters, or in the first two sets of questions in this section. The purpose here is not to give conclusive recommendations, but to raise issues which the author considers relevant to a critical appraisal of this area of intervention and its future in Latin American countries.

Justification for Further Investments

Question: Are further investments in intervention programs justified by the data now available on (1) child development in environments in which poverty and malnutrition are present, and on (2) results from intervention programs?

Answer: Before responding to this question, it is necessary to make a distinction between justification for investment on behalf of preschool children living in poverty and justification for investment in the type of intervention programs reviewed in this monograph.

In connection with the first justification, this monograph has documented that the number of preschool children living in conditions of extreme poverty in some Latin American countries is extremely large and constitutes a major public health concern. This is true not only because such conditions interfere with health and somatic growth of children, but also because, as the evidence reviewed indicates, their cognitive development may be at stake. In countries where these adverse effects are widespread, human capital has been depleted and the final cost is extremely high. In this context, it seems imperative to allocate a country's resources in such a way that the growth and development of impoverished children will be fostered in spite of their socioeconomic circumstances.

On the other hand, it has not been clearly established that the intervention programs in question are effective enough to justify large investments. The information now available on the functional adequacy of these programs is insufficient to allow the assumption that they will be successful in large-scale national programs. Nonetheless, it must be emphasized that these data, if used wisely, could serve as the bases for decisions on action. There are probably few other areas of intervention on behalf of children which have accumulated as much information for the prevention or amelioration of cognitive derangements among impoverished preschool children.

Question: What additional information would be necessary before a decision could be taken to implement large-scale programs?

Answer: One of the most surprising findings in this review has been the similarity in results among studies using different intervention strategies. Although these results reflect the plasticity of the developing organism, they do not necessarily imply that all the observed upward changes occurred at the same organismic level. While some changes may be deep-rooted and sustained over time, others may be easily reversible. These possibilities emphasize the need for an assessment of sustenance of effects. This is particularly important if the programs are to feed into a formal educational system which is unsatisfactory and which may not maintain the early gains.

Associated with the above is the general issue of inputs into the interventions. It appears that comprehensive intervention, as previously defined (a combination of nutrition, health, and psycho-educational stimulation), is the most effective intervention strategy; however, the information on this issue is too limited to warrant conclusive inferences. Given the cost of comprehensive programs, it is imperative to determine, for example, whether approaches directed to the broadening and solidification of parental caretaking practices bring about results similar to those obtained through comprehensive programs. The issue of comprehensiveness must be evaluated in the context of the degree of poverty or biosocial deprivation of the recipients. In conditions of extreme poverty, a comprehensive approach may be the only solution; all other alternatives may be inapplicable.

In connection with timing of the intervention, it is also necessary to document further the developmental stages at which the intervention is most effective and when it is no longer useful. This information may well dictate the duration and, consequently, the cost of a program over a period of time.

Precise definitions of the functional gains of these programs are also required; functional strategy may spell out the benefits of these programs in terms that can be compared with cost and investment. Initially, this stance may appear devoid of humanistic perspective but, unfortunately, in the context of resource allocation, such terminology is necessary in order to provide the children with developmental necessities.

Question: Do the needs of children in Latin America and the search for effective interventions justify further investment in quasi-experimental studies?

Answer: The quasi-experimental studies described in Chapter 4 were academic undertakings which investigated the complex interrelationships between malnutrition, poverty, and mental development. In some cases, as the research unfolded, the investigators became involved in social policy considerations, especially in connection with their own modes of intervention. These involvements, however, were probably by-products of their investigative work.

From a strictly academic perspective, quasi-experimental studies such as those reviewed are totally legitimate. Indeed, their very nature shows the ways in which interdisciplinary endeavors, including social and biological sciences, can aid in the understanding of the growth and development of the human organism. It is far from clear, however, whether studies built on a strict research infrastructure, such as the quasi-experimental studies reviewed, make a significant contribution to the solution of the problems of the children they study. Moreover, in the specific case of intervention strategies, it is even more questionable whether the data generated by these studies can be generalized to programs whose aim is service and not research.

Social science research that attempts to meet the demands of aseptic experimentation must come as close as possible to laboratory conditions. The questions or hypotheses they formulate, as in the studies in question, gain in merit as they approximate universal generalizability. Thus, they avoid being situation-bound, that is, within the limits of what is ethically and mechanically permissible. To do so they must lose sight, at least partially, of some of the cultural, social, and economic idiosyncrasies which make the groups unique. Interventions (that is, day care centers, food supplementation) built on the type of research structure described above may create the illusion of replicability. To the observer, the overt mechanics of the intervention, rather than the bases that support the operation, are the focus of attention. Moreover, interested parties often interpret the results of such aseptic intervention not in the context of its universal goals, but in the context of specific target groups and the idiosyncrasies which characterise them. Large error factors are to be expected in the transfer of this type of intervention.

The kinds of research undertakings required on the developmental needs of Latin American children and on intervention programs designed for their benefit demand a situation-bound approach. Investigators must immerse themselves in the ecology, culture, and socioeconomic characteristics of the groups under study in order to grasp or define clearly the specific nature of the research problem. For example, a study of malnutrition causality, undertaken to identify points of intervention among Indian communities in the province of Cotopaxi, Ecuador, will require a study design which thoroughly examines the physical, anthropological, and sociological conditions of this Andean population (Varea Teran, 1974). This degree of specificity, which here is called situation-bound experimentation, has an applied goal rather than a strictly scientific one. Programs developed to determine universal characteristics of malnutrition causality are unlikely to utilize similar designs.

The situation with regard to intervention research is perhaps even more clear. It has been noted repeatedly in this monograph that interventions within the framework of research do not operate in the same manner as those within the framework of service. Thus, the transfer of operation strategies from research to service frequently is unsuccessful. It appears, therefore, that the most desirable approach to effective intervention begins with a pilot study which includes the essential characteristics of the large service project which is the eventual goal.

Facilitating the Implementation of Programs

Question: It is apparent from the review of programs that with very few exceptions (that is, Puno, Peru), intervention programs were initiated and implemented in specific communities or regions without previous assessments of wants or needs. Are there dangers in this approach? Are there alternatives?

Answer: Research data reviewed in this monograph have shown that even within a particular community there may be wide variations in the social conditions of families and in the nutritional and health status of children. Variations of this nature are likely to be larger between communities with similar per capita income or similar educational levels among adults. These data, and what is known of the sociology of poverty, indicate that while different populations display common economic indicators of poverty, they will also display important differences in health status, family characteristics and organization, forms of life, attitudes, and beliefs. For example, point prevalence of protein-energy malnutrition among children may vary significantly between communities which are geographically close to one another and have similar per capita income. Thus, in one community a dietary input may be a necessary component in a childhood intervention program, while in the other it may represent only a desirable addition.

Another example in the social realm is pertinent. Hypothetically, urban populations may be more willing than rural populations to separate mother and infant and allow the latter to be enrolled in a day care center. With this arrangement urban mothers may have the opportunity to join the working force; this is less likely to be the case with rural mothers. Thus a day care center for infants and toddlers may be implemented more easily and may function more successfully in an urban, rather than a rural, setting.

Up to the present time there has been little concern for, or research on, characteristics of the populations in which intervention programs have been the most successful. To some extent, this absence of information has contributed to the lack of analysis of the ways in which community characteristics determine the degree of program success. In addition, because no information is available on the function of such analyses, little work has been done in Latin America on the ways in which data on population characteristics should be used in planning long-term programs. As in health and nutrition planning, a data base is required for program planning in order to specify needs and formulate ad hoc recommendations for selected populations or regions.

Question: Can these programs be amenable to cost-benefit analyses?
If so, will such analyses facilitate their implementation?
Answer: A key issue in connection with this question is whether social programs which may not yield tangible or quantifiable benefits should be subject to economic analysis. Specifically, is it possible to measure in economic units the impact of protecting and fostering the intellectual competence of a child during his life span?

These considerations notwithstanding, it must be recognized that, in the context of resource allocation from limited budgets, it will be necessary to subject these programs to cost-benefit analysis. This is particularly the case if, as in Colombia and Chile, the end goal is to incorporate these programs into government planning and activity. Efforts in this direction have been made and, although the data on which such analyses were done leave much to be desired, they stand as pioneering work (BID/ODEPLAN, 1977).

Proxies for the benefits of the programs must be developed and must recognize that a one-to-one correspondence between them and the benefits will never be realized. For example, in Chile schooling benefits and participation of the mothers in the work force were used as outcome variables in the cost-benefit analysis of their program for integrative attention (BID/ODEPLAN, 1977). These and other indicators must be explored further and must be tested so that tight economic analysis of these interventions will be feasible (for example, Woodhall, 1970). One of the most demanding investigations remains to be done in Latin America. A methodology must be constructed for developing low-cost interventions that takes into account the needs of children and that estimates what can be achieved within a specified time frame. Such an endeavor obviously requires a multidisciplinary team of social scientists. The task is not only possible, but may yield enormous benefits for children in Latin America.

BIBLIOGRAPHY

Agualimpia, C. 1969. "Demographic Facts of Colombia." Milbank
Memorial Fund Quarterly 47:255.

Aguilera, J. A. 1975. La Población de Venezuela. Caracas,
Venezuela: Universidad Central de Venezuela.

Aguirrezabal, I., C. DeTrujillo, and B. Botero. 1976. El Plan
de Desarrollo López, II. Controversia. Bogotá, Colombia:
Centro de Investigación y Educación Popular.

Ahluwalia, M. S. 1975. "Income Inequality: Some Dimensions of
the Problem." In Redistribution with Growth, by H. Chevery,
M. S. Ahluwalia, C. L. G. Bell, J. H. Duloy, and R. Jolly.
London: World Bank, Oxford University Press.

Banco Obrero. 1972. Política de Vivienda, Caracas: Banco Obrero.
Presented at UPADI convention in Lima, Peru, October.

Barreda-Moncada, G. 1963. Estudios Sobre Alteraciones del
Crecimiento y del Desarrollo Psicológico del Síndrome Pluri-
carencial (Kwashiorkor). Caracas, Venezuela: Editora Grafas.

Bengoa, J. M. 1976. Salud Materno Infantil y Bienestar Familiar.
Chapter: Nutrición Materno-Infantil. Caracas, Venezuela:
Instituto Nacional de Nutrición.

Bernard van Leer Foundation. 1976a. Advisory Mission to Colombia on Early Childhood Education: Report. The Hague, Nether-
lands. Mimeographed.

———. 1976b. Advisory Mission on Early Childhood Education:
Profile on and Introduction to Colombia. The Hague, Nether-
lands. Mimeographed.

Berrueta-Clements, J., A. Flores, and C. Aurora. 1977. Visita
el Programa de Hogares de Cuidado Diario. Cartagena, Colombia: Oficina de Rehabilitacion de Tugurios. Mimeographed.

Berry, J. W. 1974. "Radical Cultural Relativism and the
Concept of Intelligence." In Culture and Cognition: Readings

in Cross-Cultural Psychology, edited by J. W. Berry and P. R. Dasen. New York: Harper and Row.

————. 1976. Human Ecology and Cognitive Style. Comparative Studies in Cultural and Psychological Adaptation. New York: Halsted.

Berry, R. A., and M. Urrutia. 1976. Income Distribution and Government Policy in Colombia. New Haven: Yale University Press.

BID/ODEPLAN. 1977. Atención Integral a Menores en Extrema Pobreza Urbana. Programa de Adiestramiento en la Preparación y Evaluación de Proyectos. Santiago, Chile: Oficina de Planificacion Nacional.

Birch, H. E., C. Pineiro, E. Alcalde, T. Toca, and J. Cravioto. 1971. "Relation of Kwashiorkor in Early Childhood and Intelligence at School Age." Pediatric Research 5:579.

Borges Ramos, H. E., ed. 1977. "Situación Sanitario-Asistencial del Pre-Escolar Venezolano." II. Jornadas de Estudio del Pre-Escolar en Venezuela. Caracas, Venezuela.

Borges Ramos, H. L., ed. 1977. "Cuestiones Médicas. Programas y Proyectos." II. Jornadas de Estudio del Pre-Escolar en Venezuela. Caracas, Venezuela.

Brockman, L., and H. Ricciuti. 1971. "Severe Protein-Calorie Malnutrition and Cognitive Development in Infancy and Early Childhood." Developmental Psychology 4:312.

Bronfenbrenner, U. 1974. Is Early Intervention Effective? U.S. Department of Health, Education and Welfare. DHEW Publication no. (OHD) 76-30025. Washington, D.C.

Burton, J. H. 1976. "Problems of Child Health in a Peruvian Shanty Town." Tropical Doctor 6:81.

Campbell, D. T., and J. C. Stanley. 1973. Experimental and Quasi-Experimental Designs for Research. Chicago: Rand McNally.

Castillo, R. C. 1975. Los Niños del Perú. Clases Sociales, Ideología y Política. Lima, Perú: Editorial Universo.

CEDEN/FEPEC. 1976. Desarrollo de Niños de 0-24 Meses a Través de un Modelo de Educación No Formal en Nutrición, Salud, y Estimulación. Bogotá, Colombia: Fundación para la Educación Permanente en Colombia (FEPEC).

CEDEN/FEPEC. 1977a. Desarrollo Infantil y Educación No Formal: Diseño y Progreso de un Estudio Piloto. Bogotá, Colombia.

CEDEN/FEPEC. 1977b. Prevalencia de la Desnutrición. Brecha Alimentaria y Desarrollo Mental. Bogotá, Colombia.

CELADE. 1978. Boletin Demografico 22. Santiago, Chile.

Centro de Investigación y Desarrollo de la Educación. 1976. Proyecto Padres Hijos: (1) Informe Histórico; (2) Presentación Resumida; (3) Una Investigación en Acción en el Área Rural de Limache y San Felipe. Santiago, Chile.

Chavez, A., and C. Martinez. 1979. "Consequences of Insufficient Nutrition on Child Character and Behavior." In Malnutrition Environment and Behavior. New Perspectives, edited by D. Levitsky. Ithaca, N.Y.: Cornell University Press.

Chavez, A., and C. Martinez. 1979. Nutrición y Desarrollo Infantil. Mexico D. F.: Interamericana, Mexico.

Chen, Chi-Yi. 1970. Los Pobladores de Caracas y su Procedencia. Caracas, Venezuela: Editorial Arte.

Christiensen, N., L. Vuori, J. Clement, J. O. Mora, and A. Florez. 1977a. "Effects of an Early Education Program on Caregiver-Infant Interaction." Paper presented at the Symposium on Evaluation Research and Social Policy, National Meeting of the American Sociological Association, Chicago, Illinois.

Christiensen, N., L. Vuori, J. O. Mora, and M. Wagner. 1977b. "El Ambiente Social y su Relación con la Desnutrición y el Desarrollo Mental." Educación Hoy 42:3.

CIDE. See Centro de Investigación y Desarrollo de la Educación.

Cole, M., and J. S. Bruner. 1971. "Cultural Differences and Inferences about Psychological Processes." American Psychologist 26:867.

Colombian Information Services. 1976. Colombia Regions. New York.

Coludes. 1974. Committee for the Fight Against Malnutrition. Final Report. Caracas, Venezuela.

Comision Multisectorial del Plan Nacional de Política Alimentaria y Nutricional. 1973. Perú: Situación y Politica Alimentaria y Nutricional. Lima, Perú: Instituto Nacional de Planificación.

Consejo Venezolano del Niño. 1977. Atención Integral que el Consejo Venezolano del Niño Ha Brindado al Pre-Escolar en los Últimos 10 Años. Caracas, Venezuela.

————. 1973. Familia y Abandono de Menores. Caracas, Venezuela.

Cotler, J. 1975. "The New Mode of Political Domination in Peru." In The Peruvian Experiment, edited by A. F. Lowenthal. Princeton, N.J.: Princeton University Press.

Cravioto, J., and E. R. DeLicardie. 1973. "Longitudinal Study of Language Development in Severely-Malnourished Children." In Nutrition and Mental Functions, edited by G. Servan. New York: Plenum Press.

Cravioto, J., and B. Robles. 1965. "Evolution of Adaptive and Motor Behavior During Rehabilitation from Kwashiorkor." American Journal of Orthopsychiatry 35:449.

Cravioto, J., E. R. DeLicardie, and H. G. Birch. 1966. "Nutrition, Growth and Neuro-Integrative Development: An Experimental and Ecologic Study. Pediatrics (Supplement) 38:part 2.

CVN. See Consejo Venezolano del Niño.

Daza, H. J. 1977. Transcripcion de Algunos Aspectos de Salud Encontrados en una Consulta para Acción Preventiva Integral en Niños de las Zonas Marginadas. II. Jornadas de Estudio del Pre-escolar en Venezuela. Caracas, Venezuela.

Delange, F., A. Costa, A. M. Ermans, H. K. Ibbertson, A. Queriod, and J. B. Stanbury. 1972. "A Survey of the Clinical and Metabolic Patterns of Endemic Cretinism. In Human Development and the Thyroid Gland. Relation to Endemic Cretinism, edited by J. B. Stanbury and R. L. Kroc. New York: Plenum Press.

DeLicardie, E. R., and J. Cravioto. 1974. "Behavioral Responsiveness of Survivors of Clinically-Severe Malnutrition to Cognitive Demands." In Early Malnutrition and Mental Development, edited by J. Cravioto, L. Hambreus, and B. Valhquist. Uppsala, Sweden: Almquist and Wiksel.

Departamento Administrativo de Planeación y Servicios Técnicos, Municipio de Medellín. 1977. Anuario Estadístico de Medellín. Medellín, Colombia.

Dew, E. 1969. Politics in the Altiplano: The Dynamics of Change in Rural Peru. Austin, Texas: University of Texas Press.

Dodge, P. R., H. Palkes, R. Fierro-Benitez, and I. Ramirez. 1969. "Effect on Intelligence of Iodine in Oil Administered to Young Andean Children. A Preliminary Report." In Endemic Goiter: Report of the Meeting of the PAHO Scientific Group on Endemic Goiter, Mexico, 1968, edited by J. B. Stanbury. PAHO Scientific Publication, no. 193:378. Washington, D.C.

Drysdale, R. S. 1972. "Factores Determinantes de la Deserción Escolar en Colombia." Revista del Centro de Estudios Educativos 2:3.

———. 1974. "Flujo Estudiantil en las Escuelas Primarias de Colombia." Revista del Centro de Estudios Educativos 3:33.

Drysdale, R. S., and R. Myers. 1975. "Continuity and Change: Peruvian Education." In The Peruvian Experiment, edited by A. F. Lowenthal. Princeton, N.J.: Princeton University Press.

Dunn, J. T. 1972. "The Effects of Thyroid Hormone on Protein Synthesis in the Central Nervous System of Developing Mammals." In Human Development and the Thyroid Gland. Relation to Endemic Cretinism, edited by J. B. Stanbury and R. L. Kroc. New York: Plenum Press.

Duran de Vargas, I., ed. 1977. Una Experiencia de "Aula Abierta." Caracas, Venezuela: Fundación Mendoza.

Eskenasy, S. P. 1978. Review of Intervention Programs for Pre-Schoolers in Venezuela. Master's dissertation, Massachusetts Institute of Technology.

Federación de Instituciones Privadas de Asistencia al Niño. 1974. Educación Familiar—Evaluación de un Programa Piloto. Caracas, Venezuela.

——. 1975a. Federación de Instituciones Privadas de Asistencia al Niño. Pamphlet. Caracas, Venezuela.

——. 1975b. Estatutos (Reforma del 20 de Junio de 1975). Caracas, Venezuela.

——. 1976. Programa de Educación Familiar Pre-Escolar: Instructivo Para el Maestro de Aula. Caracas, Venezuela.

Fierro-Benitez, R., I. Ramirez, E. Estrella, C. Jaramillo, C. Diaz, and J. Urresta. 1969. "Iodized Oil in the Prevention of Endemic Goiter and Associated Defects in the Andean Region of Ecuador: I. Program Design, Effects on Goiter Prevalence, Thyroid Function and Iodine Excretion." In Endemic Goiter, edited by J. B. Stanbury. Report of the Meeting of the PAHO Scientific Group on Endemic Goiter, Mexico. PAHO, Scientific Publication no. 193:306. Washington, D.C.

Fierro-Benitez, R., I. Ramirez, E. Estrella, and J. B. Stanbury. 1974. "The Role of Iodine in Intellectual Development in an Area of Endemic Goiter." In Endemic Goiter and Cretinism: Continuing Threats to World Health, edited by J. T. Dunn and G. A. Medeiros-Neto. PAHO, Scientific Publication no. 292. Washington, D.C.

Filp, J., C. Balmaceda, M. Bastias, S. Iglesias, P. Jimeno, E. Parraguez, L. Tores, C. Tanez, and J. Zuleta. 1977. "El Proyecto Padres e Hijos: Educación Familiar Para el Desarrollo del Niño Pre-Escolar." In Seminario Internacional Sobre Estimulación Psico-Social Precoz del Lactante y Pre-Escolar. Proceedings of a Conference. Santiago, Chile.

FIPAN. See Federación de Instituciones Privadas de Asistencia al Niño.

Fisk, D., M. Adams, and J. Evans. 1977. Final Report on a Consulting Visit to Lima and Puno, Peru, September-October, 1976. Ypsilanti, Michigan: High/Scope Educational Research Foundation.

Frank, C. R., and R. Webb. 1977. "An Overview of Income Distribution in Less Developed Countries: Policy Alternatives and Design." In Income Distribution and Growth in the Less Developed Countries, edited by C. R. Frank and R. Webb. Washington, D.C.: The Brookings Institution.

Freire, P. 1973. Education for Critical Consciousness. New York: The Seabury Press.

———. 1970. Pedagogy of the Oppressed. New York: The Seabury Press.

Frisancho, R., J. E. Klayman, and J. Matos. 1976. "Symbiotic Relationship of High Fertility, High Childhood Mortality and Socioeconomic Status in an Urban Peruvian Population." Human Biology 48:101.

Fundacion de Jardines Infantiles. 1977. Plaza Pre-Escolar. Santiago, Chile.

Fundacion Festival del Nino. 1977. Políticas de la Fundación del Niño. Caracas, Venezuela.

———. 1976a. Programa Centros Pre-Escolares. Caracas, Venezuela.

———. 1976b. Programa Hogares de Cuidado Diario—Coordinación Educativa. Caracas, Venezuela.

———. 1976c. Programa Hogares de Cuidado Diario—Coordinación General. Caracas, Venezuela.

———. 1976d. Programa Hogares de Cuidado Diario—Coordinación Legal. Caracas, Venezuela.

———. 1976e. Programa Hogares de Cuidado Diario—Coordinación Social. Caracas, Venezuela.

Fundación Mendoza. 1977. "Capítulo Psico-Pedagógico." II. Jornadas de Estudio del Pre-Escolar en Venezuela. Caracas, Venezuela.

———. 1972. Educación Pre-Escolar en Venezuela. Caracas, Venezuela: Editoriales Cromotip.

———. 1976a. "Educación Pre-Escolar—Área Psico-Pedagógica. Programas y Proyectos 1966-1976." II. Jornadas de Estudio del Pre-Escolar en Venezuela. Caracas, Venezuela.

———. 1976b. La Obra de la Fundación Eugenio Mendoza al Servicio del Pre-Escolar en Venezuela. Caracas, Venezuela.

———. 1966. El Pre-Escolar en Venezuela. Caracas, Venezuela: Editorial Sucre.

Gall, N. 1974. Peru's Education Reform. I-IV. New Hampshire: American University Field Staff Studies.

Galofré, F. 1979. Pobreza y los Primeros Años de la Niñez. Situación en America Latina y el Caribe. Santiago, Chile: CEPAL.

Geber, M., and R. F. A. Dean. 1956. "The Psychological Changes Accompanying Kwashiorkor. Courrier 6:3.

Gobernacion de Antioquía. Anuario 1976 Estadístico de Antioquía. República de Colombia.

Gomez, F., R. Ramos, S. Frank, J. Cravioto, R. Chavez, and J. Vasquez. 1956. "Mortality in Second and Third Degree Malnutrition." Journal of Tropical Pediatrics 2:77.

Graham, G. C., and E. Morales. 1963. "Studies in Infantile Malnutrition. I. Nature of the Problem in Peru." Journal of Nutrition 79:479.

Graves, P. L. 1978. "Nutrition and Infant Behavior: A Replication Study in Katmandu Valley, Nepal." American Journal of Clinical Nutrition 31:541.

———. 1976. "Nutrition, Infant Behavior and Maternal Characteristics: A Pilot Study in West Bengal, India." American Journal of Clinical Nutrition 29:305.

Greene, L. S. 1977. "Hyperendemic Goiter, Cretinism, and Social Organization in Highland Ecuador." In Malnutrition, Behavior and Social Organization, edited by L. S. Greene. New York: Academic Press.

Gross, D. R., and B. A. Underwood. 1972. "Technological Changes and Calorie Costs: Sisal Agriculture in Northeastern Brazil." American Anthropologists 73:725.

Hall, J. W. 1972. "Verbal Behavior as a Function of Amount of Schooling." American Journal of Psychology 85:277.

Halpern, R. 1977. A Case of Investment in Early Intervention: Initial Education in Peru. Ph.D. dissertation, Florida State University.

Handelman, H. 1975. Struggle in the Andes. Peasant Political Mobilization in Peru. Austin, Texas: The University of Texas Press.

Harbison, F. H. 1977. "The Education-Income Connection." In Income Distribution and Growth in the Less Developed Countries, edited by C. R. Frank and R. C. Webb. Washington, D.C.: The Brookings Institution.

Havinghurst, R. J. 1973. La Sociedad y la Educación en América Latina. Argentina: Editorial Universitaria de Buenos Aires.

Hertzig, M. E., H. G. Birch, S. A. Richardson, and J. Tizard. 1972. "Intellectual Levels of School Children Severely Malnourished During the First Two Years of Life." Pediatrics 49:814.

Hoxeng, J. 1973. Let Jorge Do It. Amherst, Mass.: University of Massachusetts, Center for International Education.

Hunt, J. V. 1976. "Environmental Risk in Fetal and Neonatal Life and Measured Infant Intelligence." In Origins of Intelligence, edited by M. Lewis. New York: Plenum Press.

ICBF. See Instituto Colombiano de Bienestar Familiar.

IDB. See Inter American Development Bank.

INN. 1977. Encuesta Nutricional del Pre-Escolar. Caracas, Venezuela.

Instituto Colombiano de Bienestar Familiar. 1977. Atención Integral. Bogotá, Colombia (documento de trabajo).

———. 1976. Ley No. 27 de 1974. Bogotá, Colombia.

———. No date. "Subdirección de Asistencia Legal." Ley 75 de 1968. Bogotá, Colombia.

Instituto Colombiano de Bienestar Familiar Regional de Antioquía. 1977. La Ley 27 de 1974 Como Instrumento de Promoción de la Mujer a Través de sus Hijos Menores de 7 Anos. Medellín, Colombia.

———. 1975. Estudio Para la Localización de los Centros de Atención Integral al Pre-Escolar en Medellín. Medellín, Colombia.

Inter American Development Bank. 1975. Economic and Social Progress in Latin America. Annual Report. Washington, D.C.

Irwin, M., P. Engle, C. Yarbrough, R. Klein, and J. Townsend. 1978. "The Relationship of Prior Ability and Family Characteristics to School Attendance and School Achievement in Rural Guatemala." Child Development 49:415.

Jurisdicción de Menores. 1976. Ley 83 de 1946. Entrega no. 30. Bogotá, Colombia.

Klein, R., H. Freeman, J. Kagan, C. Yarbrough, and J. P. Habicht. 1972. "Is Big Smart? The Relation of Growth to Cognition." Journal of Health and Social Behavior 13:219.

Klein, R. E., P. Arenales, H. Delgado, G. Engle, G. Guzmán, M. Irwin, A. Lechtig, R. Martorell, V. Mejía Pivaral, P. Rusell, and C. Yarbrough. 1977. "Efectos de la Nutrición Materna Sobre el Crecimiento Fetal y el Desarrollo del Niño." Boletín de la Oficina Sanitaria Panamericana 83:24.

Lappe, F. M., and J. Collins. 1977. Food First Beyond the Myth of Scarcity. Boston: Houghton Mifflin.

Lechtig, A., J. P. Habicht, H. Delgado, R. E. Klein, C. Yarbrough, and R. Martorell. 1975. "Effect of Food Supplementation During Pregnancy on Birth Weight." Pediatrics 56:508.

Leibel, R., D. Greenfield, and E. Pollitt. 1979. "Biochemical and Behavioral Aspects of Sideropenia." British Journal of Hematology 41:145-50.

Lester, B., R. Klein, and S. Martinez. 1975. "The Use of Habituation in the Study of the Effects of Infantile Malnutrition." Developmental Psychobiology 8:541.

Lira, M. I., and S. Folch. 1978. Manuales de Estimulación. Santiago, Chile: Editorial Galdoc LTDA.

Lira, M. I., and S. Rodriguez. 1976. "Estudios Realizados con la Escala de Evaluación del Desarrollo Psicomotor. b) Desarrollo Psicomotor de Lactantes de Santiago: Diferencias Según Áreas de Desarrollo en Dos Niveles Socioeconomicos." In Escala de Evaluación del Desarrollo Psicomotor 0 a 24 Meses. Santiago, Chile.

Llanos, Z. M. 1974. El Funcionamiento Intelectual de los Niños en las Zonas Marginales de Lima. Montevideo, Uruguay: Instituto Interamericano del Niño.

Llanos, Z. M., and O. Flores. 1976. Evaluación del Proyecto Experimental de Educación Inicial no Escolarizada de Puno. Lima, Perú: Ministerio de Educación.

Loreto de Perez, B., O. Chávez de Romero, and L. T. Fermin. 1976. Proyecto Para la Creación de un Módulo de Evaluación en un Centro Pre-Escolar. Caracas, Venezuela: Ministerio de Educación.

Lowenthal, A., ed. 1975. The Peruvian Experiment: Continuity and Changes Under Military Rule. Princeton, N.J.: Princeton University Press.

Majluf, A. 1974. Continuación y Ampliación del Programa de Estimulación Para Niños de Pueblos Jóvenes que Evidencian Inmadurez Para el Aprendizaje. Mimeographed.

————. 1972. Programa Experimental de Estimulación Para Niños de 5 Años de los Pueblos Jóvenes de Lima que Evidencian Inmadurez Para el Aprendizaje. Mimeographed.

————. 1971. Madurez Para el Aprendizaje de los Niños de 5 Años de las Zonas Marginales (Pueblos Jóvenes) de Lima. Mimeographed.

Marcondes, E., A. Lefevre, D. Machado, N. Garcia de Barros, A. Vacallo, S. Gazal, G. Quarentei, N. Setian, M. Valente, and D. Barbieri. 1973. "Neuropsychomotor Development and Pneumonencephalographic Changes in Children with Severe Malnutrition." Environmental and Child Health 19:135.

Mariategui, J. C. 1971. 7 Ensayos de Interpretación de la Realidad Peruana. Lima, Perú: Biblioteca Amauta.

Marshall, C. L., and C. L. Paul. 1970. "Reduced Population Growth as Related to the Urbanization Process: Medellín, Colombia." Clinical Pediatrics 9:736.

Matovinovic, J., M. A. Child, M. Z. Nichaman, and F. L. Trowbridge. 1974. "Iodine and Endemic Goiter." In Endemic Goiter and Cretinism: Continuing Threats to World Health, edited by J. T. Dunn and G. A. Medeiros-Neto. PAHO, Scientific Publication no. 292. Washington, D.C.

McCall, R. B. 1979. "The Development of Intellectual Functioning in Infancy and the Prediction of Later IQ." In Handbook of Infant Development, by J. Osofsky. New York: Wiley.

—. 1977. "Toward an Epigenetic Conception of Mental Development in the First Three Years of Life." In Origin of Intelligence. New York: Plenum.

McCance, R. A., and E. M. Widdowson. 1966. "Protein Deficiencies and Caloric Deficiencies." Lancet 2:158.

McKay, H., L. Sinisterra, A. McKay, H. Gomez, and P. Lloreda. 1978. "Improving Cognitive Ability in Chronically Deprived Children." Science 200:270.

McLaren, D. S. 1966. "A Fresh Look at Protein-Calorie Malnutrition." Lancet 2:485.

Millikan, M., and D. Hapgood. 1967. No Easy Harvest: The Dilemma of Agriculture in Underdeveloped Countries. Cambridge, Mass.: MIT Press.

Ministerio de Educación. 1977. Dirección de Educación Especial. Caracas, Venezuela: Servicios de Educación Especial.

—. 1974. Programa de Educación Pre-Escolar. Edición Oficial. Caracas, Venezuela: Dirección General del Ministerio de Educación.

Ministerio de Educación/Perú. 1976. Estadisticas de la Educación: 1976. Lima, Perú: Oficina Sectorial de Estadistica.

—. 1975. Guia de Programas No Escolarizados de Educación Inicial. Lima, Perú.

———. 1972. Ley General de Educación. Decreto Ley. No. 19326.

Ministry of Education. 1976. Memoria y Cuenta. Caracas, Venezuela.

Monckeberg, F. 1968. "Effect of Early Marasmic Malnutrition on Subsequent Physical and Psychological Development." In Malnutrition, Learning and Behavior, edited by N. S. Scrimshaw and J. Gordon. Cambridge, Mass.: MIT Press.

Monckeberg, F., S. Tisler, S. Toro, V. Gattas, and L. Vegas. 1972. "Malnutrition and Mental Development." The American Journal of Clinical Nutrition 25:766.

Montenegro, H., D. Correa, I. Gallardo, F. Guerrero, C. Larrain, R. Hurtado, and M. Barrios, 1977. "Como Pueden los Adolescentes de una Comunidad Ayudar a los Niños Sin Oportunidades Pre-Escolares." Educación Hoy 7:43.

Montenegro, H., S. Rodriguez, M. Lira, I. Haeussler, and S. Bralic. 1977. Programas Piloto de Estimulación Precoz Para Niños de Nivel Socioeconómico Bajo Entre 0 y 2 Años: Informe Final. Santiago, Chile: Servicio Nacional de Salud.

Mora, J. O., B. Paredes, M. Wagner, L. deNavarro, J. Suescun, N. Christiensen, and G. M. Herrera. 1979. "Nutritional Supplementation and the Outcome of Pregnancy. I. Birthweight." American Journal of Clinical Nutrition 32:455.

Mora, J. O., L. deNavarro, J. Clement, M. Wagner, and B. de Paredes. 1978. "The Effect of Nutritional Supplementation on Calorie and Protein Intake of Pregnant Women." Nutrition Reports International 17:217.

MSAS. 1976a. Congreso Venezolano de Salud Pública. Chapters 4, 6, 7, 8, 9, 12, and 14. Caracas, Venezuela.

———. 1976b. División de Sistemas Estadísticos y de Conmutación. Caracas, Venezuela.

Nelson, W. E., V. C. Vaughan, and R. J. McKay. 1969. Textbook of Pediatrics. 9th ed. Philadelphia: Saunders.

Oficina Nacional de Estadística y Censo. República del Perú. 1974. Perú: Crecimiento Demográfico y Desarrollo Económico y Social. Lima, Perú.

Ohlin, G. 1967. Population Control and Economic Development. Paris: OECD.

OMEP. 1974. "Mesa Redonda Sobre Experiencias Venezolanas en Educación Pre-Escolar." XIV Congreso Mundial de Educación Pre-Escolar. Caracas, Venezuela.

Organización Panamericana de la Salud. 1976. Política Nacional de Alimentación y nutrición. Publicación Cientifica no. 328. Washington, D.C.

Osio Sandoval, M. A., et al. 1976. "Hacia una Politica Nacional de Alimentación y Nutrición." Congreso Nacional de Salud Pública. Ponencia Política de Salud. Caracas, Venezuela: Instituto Nacional de Nutrición.

Osio Sandoval, M. A., and C. Medina Colina. 1977. Consideraciones Sobre una Politica Nacional de Nutrición y Alimentación. Caracas, Venezuela: Instituto Nacional de Nutrición.

Oski, F., and A. Honig. 1978. "The Effects of Therapy on the Developmental Scores of Iron-Deficient Infants." The Journal of Pediatrics 92:21.

Paez Franco, J. 1973. "The National Nutrition Program in Colombia." In Nutrition, National Development and Policy, edited by A. Berg, N. S. Scrimshaw, and D. L. Call. Cambridge, Mass.: MIT Press.

PAHO. See Pan American Health Organization.

Pan American Health Organization. 1974a. Health Conditions in the Americas: 1969-1972. PAHO Scientific Publication no. 287. Washington, D.C.

———. 1974b. Endemic Goiter and Cretinism: Continuing Threats to World Health. Report of the IV Meeting of the PAHO Technical Group on Endemic Goiter. PAHO Scientific Publication no. 292. Washington, D.C.

Parra Sandoval, R. 1973. Análisis de un Mito. La Educación Como Factor de la Movilidad Social en Colombia. Bogotá, Colombia: Universidad de los Andes.

Patch, R. W. 1973. La Parada. Lima, Perú: Mosca Azul.

Perez Sanin, E. 1976. Colombia: Country Profiles. New York: The Population Council.

Picon-Reategui, E. 1976. "Nutrition." In Man in the Andes: A Multidisciplinary Study of High Altitude Quechua, edited by P. T. Baker and M. Little. Stroudsburg, Penn.: Dowden, Hutchison & Ross.

Pollitt, E. 1974. Desnutrición, Pobreza e Inteligencia. Retablo de Papel. Lima, Perú: Instituto Nacional de Investigación y Desarrollo de la Educación.

————. 1973. "Behavioral Correlates of Severe Malnutrition in Man." In Nutrition, Growth and Development of North American Indian Children, edited by W. Moore, M. Silverberg, and M. Read. DHEW, Publication no. (NIH) 72-26. Washington, D.C.

————. 1972. "Desnutrición, Antecedentes Bio-Sociales y Desarrollo Cognoscitivo." Revista de Neuropsiquiatria 35:21.

Pollitt, E., D. Greenfield, and R. Leibel. 1978. "Behavioral Effects of Iron Deficiency among Preschool Children in Cambridge, Massachusetts." Federation Proceedings 37:487.

Pollitt, E., and H. Ricciuti. 1969. "Biological and Social Correlates of Stature among Children in the Slums of Lima, Peru." American Journal of Orthopsychiatry 39:735.

Pollitt, E., and C. Thomson. 1977. "Protein-Calorie Malnutrition and Behavior: A View from Psychology." In Nutrition and the Brain, Vol. 2, edited by R. Wurtman and J. Wurtman. New York: Raven Press. P. 261.

PROPEDEINE. 1976. Plan 1975-1980. Lima, Perú: Ministerio de Educación.

Puffer, R. R., and C. V. Serrano. 1973. Patterns of Child Mortality in Childhood. Pan American Health Organization. Scientific Publication no. 262. Washington, D.C.

Reed, C. H. 1975. Overview of Project—and Selected Findings. A publication on the joint research project of the Ministry of Education and USAID/Ecuador. Washington, D.C.: USAID.

Rein, M. 1970. "Problems in the Definition and Measurement of Poverty." In The Concept of Poverty, edited by P. Townsend. New York: American Elsevier Publishing.

Richardson, S. A. 1974. "The Background Histories of School Children Severely Malnourished in Infancy." Advances in Pediatrics 21:167.

Richardson, S. A., H. G. Birch, and M. E. Hertzig. 1973. "School Performance of Children Who Were Malnourished in Infancy." American Journal of Mental Deficiency 77:623.

Richardson, S., H. Birch, and C. Ragbeer. 1975. "The Behavior of Children at Home Who Were Severely Malnourished in the First Two Years of Life." Journal of Biosocial Science 7:255.

Rodriguez, S., V. Arancibia, and C. Undurraga. 1976. Escala de Evaluación del Desarrollo Psicomotor: 0 a 24 Meses. Santiago, Chile: Servicio Nacional de Salud, Seccion Salud Mental.

Rodriguez, S., and M. I. Lira. 1976. "Estudios Realizados con la Escala de Evaluación del Desarrollo Psicomotor. a) Desarrollo Psicomotor de Lactantes de Santiago: Diferencias Según Coeficientes de Desarrollo en: Dos Niveles Socioeconomicos y Ambos Sexos." In Escala de Evaluación del Desarrollo Psicomotor: 0 a 24 Meses, edited by S. Rodriguez, V. Aranciba, and C. Undurraga. Santiago, Chile: Servicio Nacional de Salud, Seccion Salud Mental.

Rueda-Williamson, R. 1974. "La prevención del Bocio Endémico y el Plan Decimal de Salud Para las Américas." Boletín de la Oficina Sanitaria Panamericana 77:486.

Scribner, S., and M. Cole. 1973. "Cognitive Consequences of Formal and Informal Education." Science 182:553.

Scrimshaw, N. S., and M. Behar. 1961. "Protein-Malnutrition in Young Children." Science 133:2039.

Selowsky, M. 1976. "A Note on Preschool Age Investment in Human Capital in Developing Countries." Economic Development and Cultural Change 24:707.

Sewell, J. W. 1977. The United States and World Development. Agenda 1977. Overseas Development Council. New York: Praeger Press.

Sharp, D., M. Cole, and C. Lave. 1979. "Education and Cognitive Development: The Evidence." From Experimental Research Monograph of the Society for Research in Child Development 178.

Solarte, F. C. 1976. "El Menor en Situación Irregular en Venezuela. Caracas, Venezuela: Universidad Central de Venezuela.

Stanbury, J. B. 1972. "The Clinical Pattern of Cretinism as Seen in Highland Ecuador. In Human Development and the Thyroid Gland. Relation to Endemic Cretinism, edited by J. B. Stanbury and R. L. Kroc. New York: Plenum Press.

Stanbury, J. 1977. "The Role of the Thyroid in the Development of the Human Nervous System." In Malnutrition, Behavior and Social Organization, edited by L. S. Greene. New York: Academic Press.

Stevenson, H. W., T. Parker, A. Wilkinson, B. Bonnevaux, and M. Gonzalez. 1978. "Schooling, Environment, and Cognitive Development: A Study in Peru." Monograph vor the Society Reserach

Stickney, R. E., I. D. Beghin, J. J. Urrutia, L. J. Mata, P. Arenales, J.-P. Habicht, A. Lechtig, and C. Yarbrough. 1976. "Systems Analysis in Nutrition and Health Planning: Approximate Model Relating Birthweight and Age to Risk of Deficient Growth." Archivos Latino-Americanos de Nutricion 26(1975):177.

Taub, H. B., K. M. Goldstein, and D. V. Caputo. 1977. "Indices of Neonatal Prematurity as Discriminators of Development in Middle Childhood." Child Development 48:797.

Toro, J. B., F. Alvarez, M. Rodriguez, and H. Aristizabal. 1977. "El Desarrollo del Niño a Través de la Familia y la Comunidad." Educación Hoy 7:87.

Townsend, P. 1970. "Introduction." In The Concept of Poverty, edited by P. Townsend. New York: American Elsevier Publishing.

UNICEF. 1975. Project Proposed for Peru: Integrated Services for Children. New York.

——. 1974. The Young Child: Approaches to Action in Developing Countries. E/ICEF/1303. New York.

——. 1973. Perú: Estudio Sobre la Infancia. Lima, Perú.

UNICEF/CEPAL. 1979. Indicators of the Situation of Children in Latin America and the Caribbean. No. 49.318. Santiago, Chile.

United Nations. 1970. Statistics on Children and Youth in Latin America. Santiago, Chile.

Universidad Central de Venezuela. 1970. Estudio de Caracas 6. Caracas, Venezuela: Ediciones Biblioteca.

USAID/Colombia. 1976. 1976 Colombian Health Sector Analysis. Bogota, Colombia.

——. 1974. 1974 Colombian Health Sector Analysis. Bogota, Colombia.

USAID/Peru. 1975. Sector Assessment Education. Lima, Peru.

Vallejo Mejía, C. 1975. La Situación Social en Colombia. Bogotá, Colombia: Centro de Investigación y Educación Popular.

Van den Berghe, P., and G. Primov. 1977. Inequality in the Peruvian Andes: Class and Ethnicity in Cuzco. Missouri: University of Missouri Press.

Varea Teran, J. 1974. Nutrición y Desarrollo en los Andes Ecuatorianos. Quito, Ecuador: Investigaciones Médico-Sociales del Ecuador.

Vásquez Márquez, J. 1975. La Realidad Educativa en Venezuela. Caracas, Venezuela: Ministerio de Educación, Dirección de Educación Pre-Escolar.

Villegas, M., and O. L. Gonzales. 1975. Estudio de Factibilidad de Ubicación de los Centros de Atención Integral al Pre-Escolar en los Municipios del Departamento de Antioquía. Medellín, Colombia: Instituto Colombiano de Bienestar Familiar Regional Antioquía.

Vuori, L., N. Christiensen, J. Clement, J. O. Mora, M. Wagner, and M. G. Herrera. 1979. "Nutritional Supplementation and the

Outcome of Pregnancy. Visual Habituation at 15 Days." American Journal of Clinical Nutrition 32(February):455.

Wagner, D. A. 1974. "The Development of Short-Term and Incidental Memory: A Cross-Cultural Study." Child Development 45:389.

Waterlow, J. C., and G. A. O. Alleyne. 1971. "Protein Malnutrition in Children: Advances in Knowledge in the Last Ten Years." Advances in Protein Chemistry 25:117.

Waterlow, J. C., and H. E. Rutishauser. 1974. "Malnutrition in Man." In Early Nutrition and Mental Development, edited by J. Cravioto, L. Hambreus, and B. Valhquist. Uppsala, Sweden: Almquist and Wiksel.

Webb, R. 1975. "Government Policy and the Distribution of Income in Peru, 1963-1973." In The Peruvian Experiment, edited by A. F. Lowenthal. Princeton, N.J.: Princeton University Press.

Webb, R., and A. Figueroa. 1975. Distribución del Ingreso en el Perú. Perú Problems 14. Lima, Perú: Instituto de Estudios Peruanos.

Weil, T. 1972. Area Handbook for Peru. Washington, D.C.: The American University Foreign Area Studies.

Whelan, G., J. Filp, S. Martinic, L. Torres, M. Bastias, and J. Zuleta. 1977. "Un Programa de Educación Familiar y Comunitaria Para el Desarrollo del Niño Rural en Chile." Educación Hoy 7:19.

WHO (World Health Organization). 1971. Joint FAO/WHO Expert Committee on Nutrition: Eighth Report. WHO Technical Reprint Series 477. Geneva.

Winick, M., and P. Rosso. 1969. "Head Circumference and Cellular Growth of the Brain in Normal and Marasmic Children." Journal of Pediatrics 74:774.

Woodhall, M. 1970. Cost-Benefit Analysis in Educational Planning. Paris: UNESCO.

World Bank. 1977. Colombia: Appraisal of an Integrated Nutrition Improvement Project. Washington, D.C.

————. 1976. Education Sector policy paper. Washington, D.C.

————. 1975. Health Sector policy paper. Washington, D.C.

Wray, J. D., and A. Aguirre. 1969. "Protein-Calorie Malnutrition in Candelaria, Colombia. 1. Prevalence: Social and Demographic Causal Factors." Journal of Tropical Pediatrics 25:76.

ABOUT THE AUTHOR

ERNESTO POLLITT is Professor of Nutrition and Behavioral Sciences at the University of Texas School of Public Health, Health Science Center, in Houston. Until 1978 he was Associate Professor of Growth and Development at the Department of Nutrition and Food Science at the Massachusetts Institute of Technology in Cambridge, Massachusetts. Dr. Pollitt has had a wide range of experience as a researcher and government consultant in Latin American countries. He has published extensively in the area of nutrition and child development. His articles have appeared in the <u>American Journal of Clinical Nutrition</u>, in the <u>Journal of Pediatrics</u>, and in <u>Early Human Development</u>. Dr. Pollitt holds a B.A. and a Professional Psychology degree from the Catholic University of Lima, Peru and a Ph.D. from Cornell University, Ithaca, New York.